Bella Duffy

Winifred Power

Vol. 1

Bella Duffy

Winifred Power
Vol. 1

ISBN/EAN: 9783337813840

Printed in Europe, USA, Canada, Australia, Japan

Cover: Foto ©Thomas Meinert / pixelio.de

More available books at **www.hansebooks.com**

A Novel.

IN THREE VOLUMES.
VOL. I.

LONDON:
RICHARD BENTLEY AND SON,
Publishers in Ordinary to Her Majesty the Queen.
1883.

CONTENTS OF VOL. I.

WINIFRED POWER.

CHAPTER I.

THE HATHERLEYS.

N that decade which began with the bombardment of Acre, and closed four years before the Crimean War, the drawing-room of Hatherley House looked very old-fashioned indeed.

For in those days, panelled walls, tiled fire-places, carved oak furniture, and blue china were indications of the owner's character. Instead of meaning that he swam with the tide, it meant that he fought against it. Instead of betraying him for a worshipper of fashion, it stamped him for a devotee of the past. And in Marleyford, where the Hatherleys had lived for generations, their furniture was as much identified with them as their hereditary nose (a handsome aquiline), or their grand ancestral manner.

Their neighbours, prosperous, cheery modern folk, quitting their own plate-glass and gilding, and arriving in that gloomy room, were straightway possessed with a solemn sense of the dignity of the Hatherley tradition. And Mary, the only daughter of the house, sitting in her statuesque beauty, her Quaker-like dress, on a straight-backed chair to receive them, seemed hardly nearer to their desires or their habits than a graven saint in a niche, or queen upon a tomb. John, too, the eldest son and the only son at home, with *his* sober, perfect attire, his faultless, marble face, and his reputation for exotic tastes, had always, even when youngest, struck people as a young man whose youth was a polite concession to the course of nature, but in no sense a period of immaturity.

While the other rich or aspirant inhabitants of the town ransacked the Herald's office for armorial bearings, and blazoned its inventions on the panels of their barouches, Mary rumbled along in a roomy chariot, with nothing but an initial on its chocolate-coloured doors. And while sons of tinkers and grandsons of tailors quitted their native town to blossom into esquires elsewhere, the Hatherleys with every successive generation struck apparently deeper roots into the soil there. They gave it to be understood that it was their pride to remain where the founder of the family had made his fortune. That which he had become, that they persisted in being ; and because his ambition had been crowned the day he bought a flourishing brewery, they professed to regard a brewery as the highest earthly possession.

A very upright, but a very stern man was the present head of the house. 'Old Mr.

Hatherley' he had been called ever since the stroke of paralysis which had laid him low, and left the greater part of the business in the hands of his son, John. He was everything which his father and grandfather had been before him, and more. A man of puritanic simplicity of life, and of rigid uniformity of conduct, he had never overlooked in his children or dependents the lightest disregard of his wishes. The Hatherleys had always been proud, clear-headed, just. All the organic qualities which had made his forefathers successful were crystallized in him. A psychologist might have wondered in what direction his children would develope, and argue badly from the fact that one of them, at least, had outraged every tradition. William, the second son, after a career of extravagance had enlisted in a West India regiment and was never mentioned. But in Marleyford psychologists were an unknown species. The good people of the little town judged exclusively from appearances, and were burdened with few theories.

And appearances were so remarkably in favour
of John and Mary Hatherley that it would
have been difficult to have any doubts as to
their future. The handsome, correct, unexceptionable brother and sister looked as
though no evil could sink deeper into them
than a fleck of dust into marble.

Mary, indeed, had had the faint beginnings
of a love affair which bore a disturbing resemblance to the impetuosity and wrong-headed-
ness of vulgar folk. She had engaged herself
to her second cousin, Ralph Mercer, a worthless spendthrift. He had been a ward of
Mr. Hatherley's; but, quickly exhausting
that gentleman's scanty store of patience, had
been dismissed from the brewery in which he
aspired to become a partner. 'What will
Miss Hatherley do?' was the source of some
curiosity when this happened.

But Miss Hatherley apparently did nothing,
only grew a little colder, a shade more reserved; and was supposed to be duly resigned.

As for John, whom he would marry was a

question to which the answer was so long in
coming that people had almost ceased to
expect it. The greater part of his neighbours
pronounced him a confirmed bachelor. He
was much over thirty, and precise to a fault;
moreover, he professed a mysterious affection
for old editions of rare books.

John's acquaintances regarded his little
library somewhat askant, or at best with the
good-humoured contempt of people who are
virtuously conscious of no definite superiority
in themselves. And it was remarked that the
young man never aired his archaic scholarship
in presence of his father. Mr. Hatherley was
not a man to tolerate nonsense; that was well
known. The best thing John had to do was
to stick to the brewery, his skill in the
management of which had proved him a chip
of the old block.

One evening the Hatherleys were expecting
guests to dinner. They gave solemn enter-
tainments at regularly recurring intervals, and
continued the practice even after Mr. Hatherley

became an invalid. The large, low drawing-room was lighted with wax candles in silver sconces, while the gloom was further and still more picturesquely dissipated by the ruddy blaze of a glorious fire. Mary, seated by the hearth, was staring in silence—a somewhat moody silence, as it seemed—at the changing shapes in the glowing depths of heat. Every now and again her slender hands, clasped lightly together on her lap, moved restlessly, and her straight black brows met in a frown. Clearly her meditations were not pleasing. Opposite to her, blinking in a purblind, adoring, speechless way, like a superannuated King Charles, was Martha Freake.

Not that she was old, poor Martha, only her air was so humble and depressed, her face so crumpled with anxiety and love, her attire so dowdy, that she looked old. She was the Hatherleys' poor relation and housekeeper, and had lived with them since Mary had been left a motherless baby.

' Don't look so miserable, darling: it breaks

my heart,' she ventured to say, after a pause of sorrowful watching.

Mary shrugged her shoulders petulantly. ' How can I help looking miserable, when I remember the state in which I saw him?' she retorted. Her tone was resentful, not to say sullen, and Martha quivered under it with an evident fear of having offended.

Before she could speak again, the door opened to admit John. In evening-dress he looked more majestic and unexceptionable than ever. ' Good-evening,' he said, in mellow, measured tones, as he walked forward and established himself on the hearth-rug.

Both ladies responded, Mary almost inaudibly and without raising her head; Martha with a furtive, half-guilty glance.

' You have been to London?' said the latter, noticing that the young lady was not inclined to speak.

' Yes,' answered John. ' I heard of a Hague edition of Molière with original illustrations, and hurried up to buy it.'

'And it took you three days to complete the purchase?' asked Mary suddenly; so suddenly that the question sounded like a challenge.

John pulled down his spotless cuffs, and flicked a speck of dust from the sleeve of his coat.

'I had other business, but it was less important,' he calmly replied.

'Business is an elastic term,' continued Mary, while Martha turned pale and cast to her a look of imploring deprecation. 'Whenever men are bored at home, or have something to do which they do not care to talk about, it is easy to discover the necessity for a little trip " on business." '

She did not speak the words angrily, for the Hatherley manner was usually calm; nevertheless, in her tone there ran a sound which might have been described as spite.

John smiled, but not genially.

'You speak with a certainty that would

almost suggest some personal experience of such little " business trips." But naturally the idea is absurd—since you are not a man.'

Not another word was spoken, until the butler threw open the door, announcing the Rector and his wife, ' Mr. and Mrs. Stratton;' close upon the heels of whom followed ' Mr. and Mrs. Ormerod,' and ' Mr. Russell.'

Mr. Ormerod was a banker, *the* banker of Marleyford, and Walter Russell was his nephew. The latter, a refined, intelligent-looking young man, had, as was well known, at one time proposed to Mary. Anyone watching him closely now as he wished her ' Good-evening,' would have guessed that he was still in love with her, but she showed not the faintest sign of any feeling—unless it were a little added weariness.

' We were almost afraid this morning that we should not be able to come, for Mrs. Ormerod received news of the illness of her brother,' said the banker's loud and cheerful tones.

'Sir Charles?' asked the Rector in a concerned voice, for Mrs. Ormerod's brother was a baronet.

'Sir Charles, yes, by Jove! Serious thing you know, especially now, when young Charles is laid up with scarlatina at school.'

During the significant little pause that followed this speech, one or two people's eyes travelled with a veiled curiosity towards Walter; who, in the event of his boy-cousin's death, would be next heir to the title. Martha looked meekly and regretfully at Mary ; but Mary gave no sign of comprehension.

'I hope you had better news later in the day?' said Mr. Stratton.

'Somewhat better. I went by rail into Canterbury to get the despatch. No necessity in these days to wait twenty-four hours for news. We shall soon have a wire here, I am told ; and a good thing too.'

'I have never used the telegraph yet,' remarked John.

'Oh, you are a Tory to the backbone, my dear fellow. As much behind the age as—as'
— ('your furniture,' the laughing Mr. Ormerod was just about to add, but checked himself)—'as if you were your own grandfather, by Jove!'

John smiled gravely. To a Hatherley such an accusation was a compliment, and the banker knew it.

'Mr. John lives at home, and has all his dear ones near him,' observed Mrs. Ormerod, who had something of a languishing air. 'He does not yet know the anxieties, any more than the joys of a family.'

'And you all think that he never will— don't you?' asked Mary, speaking almost for the first time, and with a sudden, slight briskness.

John cleared his throat. His air seemed to say that the conversation was growing frivolous.

'Everybody almost appears to have been to Canterbury to-day,' said the Rector. 'I was there, and so were you, Miss Hatherley, and Miss Freake.'

From John's calm eyes there flashed the faintest perceptible ray of interest. Miss Freake turned rapidly of various lively hues. Only Mary remained to all appearance unmoved.

'We went on a shopping expedition,' she replied.

'The shopping expeditions of ladies are like the business trips of men—of very frequent occurrence,' quietly put in her brother ; and the sentence had so little mean-ing to most of the hearers that they took it for a joke and laughed.

Other guests entered, and at last nine couples filed off into the dining-room, which had the same sombre and old-fashioned air as the drawing-room. The dinner was served on massive plate ; John carved, and old port circulated. The portrait of the founder of the family, clothed in municipal robes and bearing the civic chain, looked down upon the scene from his huge gold frame above the chimney-piece. He had been a handsome, striking-looking man, and it was curious to see how like John was to him— like, but 'with a difference.' The original brow was broader ; the lips were fuller ; the lines of his face, though stern, were not so rigid, and there was a fuller life behind them. John's face was like a mask, impassible, and might cover weakness as well as strength.

He was speaking of his recent purchase, Mr. Ormerod listening with a polite, half-amused smile.

'Original engravings?' he reperted. 'Ah! very interesting, I am sure. Don't know much about such things myself. Where do you pick up these books?'

'At various dealers. But often, also, from private persons. The late possessor of the Molière lived in——'

'Linden-Grove Road,' suggested Mary, from her end of the table.

'By no means. At the opposite end of London,' corrected John.

Martha, looking uneasy, quavered out in her odd, semi-senile way:

'Linden-Grove Road, Mary dear? Why, you are thinking of the neighbourhood where Parsons lives.'

'Parsons?' John asked, rather sharply.

'Don't you remember her? She was housekeeper here once, years ago. She is bedridden now, and I go to see her sometimes,' said Martha timidly.

'I am glad you go to see her,' replied John serenely, and turned with some careless remark to the lady on his right.

There was a little sleepy talk in the drawing-room later; a little mild music; Walter Russell said a few earnest words to Mary, who was looking pale and fatigued, and then at ten o'clock everybody went home.

'Mary!' began John, on returning to the drawing-room, after seeing his guests off, but Mary had already slipped away, and only Martha was left. She was obviously uneasy, and looked more deprecating than ever. Her cousin resumed :

' You were in Canterbury to-day, I hear. I need not ask the reason. Of course you went to meet Ralph Mercer.' Some surprise now succeeded to the fear on Martha's face ; never had John spoken to her on that subject in a tone so removed from irritation.

' It was partly my fault that we went,' she began, anxious still to shield her darling ; but he interrupted her with a wave of his hand.

' I ask for no explanations and wish for none. Mary knows my wishes, and those of our father. If she chooses to run counter to both, I cannot help it. But I would like you, Martha, to try to convince her that my desire—my most earnest desire—is that she would treat me with frankness ; and abandon once for all these clandestine meetings, and these paltry subterfuges which are as un- worthy of herself as insulting to me.'

Martha stared at him in the blankest

astonishment. The one point on which she had ever ventured to think John less than perfect had been his conduct in regard to his sister's engagement. For it was he, quite as much as his father, who had driven young Mercer away. Could it be that he was relenting?

John resumed :

' This Parsons ? It is strange I   not remember her.'

' She was here for a very short time in your school-days, and left to get married. Jacobs is a cousin of hers. It was through him that I first heard she was ill.'

' Jacobs?' John took up the tongs, and carefully arranged the fire. Jacobs was the butler, and had been some years in the family. The young master of Hatherley House was certainly in a very genial mood to-night, for while, as a rule, he troubled himself little about the servants, on this occasion Jacobs and Jacobs's cousin appeared to possess a singular interest for him.

'And the poor thing is bedridden, Martha? I hope she is in good circumstances?'

'Yes,' Martha said, 'her husband is a pawnbroker.'

'In the City?'

'No. In a street not very far from that Linden-Grove Road which they were speaking of at dinner.'

'Ah, yes. What a strange, absent-minded question that was of Mary's! What could have made her think that dealers in old books lived up there?' continued John, carelessly enough, but directing, nevertheless, at his companion a swift sidelong glance, which she did not see. Her thoughts were absorbed in considering how she could make John a request that, if granted, would fill Mary with joy, and earn for Martha that which she most coveted, the expression of Mary's gratitude.

She sat gazing into the fire, her breath coming quickly as the words of her petition alternately trooped to her lips ; then retreated, unuttered.

'It is late,' said John at last, rousing himself from a gloomy reverie, and eyeing her discontentedly.

Martha rose, lighted his candle, and handed it to him ; paused, and then, with a valiant rush, stammered out the words :

'John, poor Ralph is really starving.'

'Let him starve, the lazy, worthless scoundrel!' exclaimed John, with a sudden flash of fire in his eyes, before which she shrank back as scared as by the blaze of a line of guns.

Bowing her head meekly, she murmured, 'Good-night,' and crept upstairs, mortified, crestfallen, and heavy-hearted.

John retired to his library. This was a very handsome room where, installed in a high-backed chair in front of a pretentious table, he was accustomed to spend many hours, presumably in study. The people who found him there were always impressed in spite of themselves. And when the grave student, with a wave of his hand towards a quaint-looking volume in vellum, would remark that

it was an Aldine, his hearer, profoundly igno-
norant of what an Aldine might be, looked at
him with an expression curiously compounded
of contempt and awe.   With such a recondite
work open before him, John was usually discovered ; and such a work lay open upon his
table now.   Shutting it up with a brusqueness
which certes no genuine lover of old books
had   ever   used   before   him,   he thrust it
away, and sitting down upon his mediæval
chair, abandoned himself to a reverie.

Martha meanwhile had gone to Mary's room,
and found her sitting, still undressed, before
the fire.

'Did you notice ?' Mary cried exultingly,
her eyes bright with some secret triumph.

'Notice ?   What ?' asked Martha.

'His agitation when I mentioned Linden-
Grove Road ?'

Martha's hands fell to her side, and she stood
mute with surprise.

'You good old owl !' laughed Mary.   'I
believe you never saw it.'

She was quite right. Martha had not only not seen, but was still a hundred miles from comprehension.

'What does it all mean?' she asked.

'Never you mind, Patty. You are not clever at keeping secrets. They always oppress you. Suffice it to say that in future I shall know how to manage my immaculate brother.'

Too humble-minded to be inquisitive, Martha waited further information. But Mary continued to talk in riddles.

'I wonder,' she said musingly, 'if I dare pretend to know enough to extract money out of him?'

'He will not give it, I think', said Martha, and related what had passed. Mary's face fell. Either she did love this Ralph very much, or a girlish fancy had been fanned by need of excitement and the spirit of opposition into a flame.

'You could squeeze out some money for me yourself, Patty, if you chose.'

'I?' Poor Martha had nothing of her own

but a miserable £60 a-year. As generous as she was poor, she spent more than the half of it in charity or in gifts, and never had a spare sixpence by the time each quarter was a week old.

'I never knew anybody like you for being without a penny,' said Mary crossly, seeing the distress painted on her cousin's countenance. 'You have the housekeeping money. Why cannot you give me £10 out of that?'

'Mary!'

'Mary? Well, Mary what?' mocked the owner of that name with considerable peevishness.

'It would be dishonest.'

'Dishonest? Nonsense! I would give it you back next week.'

'Next week or next year, the wrong would be the same,' answered Martha softly, while a steadfast light came into her brown eyes.

'I think you are very unkind.' Martha winced but sat silent. 'Very unkind and obstinate, and puritanical and—and ridiculous,' continued the baffled beauty, and thereupon burst into tears.

A sound of angry sobbing alone broke the silence for the next few minutes. Martha was weeping also, but silently. Pale and sorrowful, she sat brushing away the tears as they coursed one by one down her cheeks, feeling herself dreadfully cruel, and yet upheld by a firm instinct of duty.

'You have often been most tiresome, Martha; but never, I think, deliberately unkind until now.'

'The refusal is—is w—worse for me to make than for y—you to hear,' wailed Martha, and broke out sobbing in her turn.

Tears are generally supposed to be a sign of weakness. Mary thought she had triumphed, and passed from reproach to entreaty. But although Martha grew damper, limper, more wretched every moment, she persisted in her resolution, and Mary ended by flying into a violent rage. Then Martha, trembling all over, crushed and mute, rose and bid her humbly 'Good-night.' She got no answer,

unless the peevish tattoo of an angry foot
could be called such. She stood for a moment
looking imploringly at the averted head of her
darling: then glided away and went down the
passage to her own room, feeling as if she
could never be happy in all her life again. Her
affections were so fresh, her heart was so pure,
her mind so simple, that harsh words and
angry looks affected her as they would a child.

For hours after she was in bed she tossed
from side to side, wondering what she could
do. At last she had an inspiration. She had
one possession of value; her mother's diamond
ring. On the morrow she would pawn that
to Parsons' husband and say nothing of her
intention until she had the money in her
hand, when she would win her pardon from
Mary's glad surprise. Enchanted, she fell
asleep at last, a smile upon her lips. Dreams
were kinder to her than men. In the magic
land of shadows the spell of fear fell from her
spirit; her faith forgot the chill of doubt, and
her own heart's music silenced discord.

CHAPTER II.

DISCOVERIES.

N reaching the station next morning to catch the train, Martha was rather surprised to find John on the same errand. His journeys to London had grown frequent of late. Formerly one a month had, on an average, been enough for him. Now, hardly a week passed without his running up. Nevertheless, Martha had not expected to see him start again on this particular morning, for it was only on the previous afternoon that he had returned after a three days' absence.

Blind as a bat, as usual, she did not notice

the slight shade of annoyance that crossed his face on perceiving her.

'Going shopping?' he inquired carelessly, as he seated himself opposite to her.

She answered ' Yes,' rather quietly: for, as we know, shopping was not the only object of her journey.

' I am bound for the City,' said he. ' I suppose your destination is Oxford Street, and you will return by the two o'clock train?'

Martha thought she was quite sure to return at two o'clock, and said so.

' That will be too early for me,' he remarked, as if the idea of accompanying her back had been the only reason of his question. And although railway speed was a much smaller thing in those days than it is in ours, he did not once again unclose his lips until the train steamed into the terminus.

Martha got through her shopping with the utmost haste, being eager to settle her business with Parsons. On descending at last from the Red Cap omnibus, and knocking at the

door of the dingy house in the little street of
shops that turned out of Linden-Grove Road,
she was startled to find herself received by a
weeping maid-of-all-work.

'What is the matter?' she asked sympathe-
tically, agitated always at the sight of trouble,
even though the sorrowful one was the grimiest
of maidens that had ever scrubbed a door-
step.

'It's the missis, ma'am. She's in a faint.
I thought you might have bin the doctor.'

'Has a doctor not been?'

'No, ma'am; but he has sent to say he is
coming. He's with a little boy in the Linden-
Grove Road, who has got convulsions.'

Martha, arriving upstairs, found the patient
surrounded by her husband and one or two
friendly female neighbours, who had resorted
to such remedies as their simple science suggested. When the doctor presently made his
appearance, Mrs. Parsons was quite sensible
again, although so pale and exhausted that he
feared a second attack. He recommended

absolute quiet ; and glanced analytically at the bystanders, with a view of discovering who among them was most likely to enforce the execution of his orders.

' *You* had better stay with her,' he said, addressing Miss Freake. ' Can you?'

'For a few hours,' she replied, making up her mind to the loss of her afternoon.

' That's right. Then I will return in an hour or two. Should there be a relapse, and you want me in a hurry, you will most likely find me close by in Linden-Grove Road, No. 14. I have a bad case there, which requires watching.'

As the illness of Mrs. Parsons has very little to do with our story, we may merely state that she had no second attack, and that about four o'clock Martha was able to leave her. Her husband, grateful to the little woman for her attention to the invalid, very quickly and liberally transacted the business of the ring, and Martha found herself the possessor of ten pounds and a pawn-ticket.

Greatly pleased with the success of her enterprise, she bid the sick woman good-bye, said a few kind words to everybody, and started forth bravely through the fog and drizzle for the Red Cap.

Her shortest way lay through Linden-Grove Road, and passing down that street, her tender heart reminded her of the little boy who, as the doctor had said, was so very ill. She began to wonder how he was, and peered about for No. 14. Not that she meant to go there, but she felt an interest in the house, knowing that a child's laughter had been hushed within its walls, and that sickness had stayed the busy tread of little feet and laid low a tiny head. 'This must be No. 14,' thought Martha, blinking through the mist. Yes—and surely that was the doctor who had just clinked open the garden-gate. He was coming away from a visit to his patient. She might give him news of Parsons, and ask him if the little boy were better.

She stopped at the gate with this intention.

But the doctor did not notice her in the uncertain light, for he was speaking to a gentleman behind him.

' And you really think I can leave him with
safety to-night ?' asked a voice, whose tones
rooted Martha to the ground with amazement.

' Indeed he is much better,' replied the
doctor. ' Not only can you leave him, but I
have impressed upon Mrs. Howard the necessity of seeking rest herself. She will break
down entirely, otherwise.'

' My wife is unfortunately of an anxious
temperament,' answered John : for John
Hatherley it was who was leaning on the
gate and saying these inconceivable things.

His wife ? Martha with difficulty suppressed an exclamation of surprise and dismay.
Surprise that John should be secretly married;
dismay at the secrecy, and the consequent
danger of detection. She shrank back into
the shadow like a guilty thing, letting the
doctor go past her unchallenged; and waited

in a kind of dream until John's receding steps
had died away upon the gravel walk.

Then she darted forward with but one idea,
that of escape ; nor did she breathe freely until
she was once more seated in the omnibus and
jolting back to the station, where she had to
wait. The stupor of her recent discovery
imprisoned her mind like a mould of lead,
affecting her hardly less than if she had found
John out in a crime. What kind of woman
could he have married ? And what would
his father, what would everybody say, when
discovery ensued ? To our simple-minded
Martha, steeped in the habits of the Hatherleys and imbued with their traditions, a clandestine marriage in connection with one of
them seemed nothing less than highly im-
proper. And how was she to behave under
the weight of this astounding mystery? The
thought of betraying John never presented
itself to her. She was as loyal as she was
loving ; and in so far as silence could shield
him, she was just as ready to stand by him

now as in the old days, when he got into
boyish scrapes, and her indulgent protection
alone averted the birch. But surreptitious
visits to the jam-closet are one thing; a
family hidden away in a remote suburb of
London is another; and Martha nearly
groaned aloud as she realized that all she
could do for John now, her dear cousin, was
to suffer for him in agonized silence and
suspense.

Lest such feelings should seem exaggerated,
it must be remembered that among the many
believers in the Hatherley 'legend,' the
staunchest, the most fervent, the most un-
questioning, was Martha. No single thing
ought to threaten the foundations of that rock
of respectability: yet a clandestine connection implies something disgraceful.

She felt quite worn out with perplexity
when she reached home at last, and was fairly
past deriving any delight even from bestowing
her £10 upon Mary.

'Where did you get it?' asked that young

lady, surprise predominating over every other sentiment.

Martha, unable to fib, but blushing at the confession, ramblingly recounted how she had pawned her mother's ring. Mary was touched, but not deeply, being accustomed to Martha's devotion.

'John has been to London again to-day,' said Mary, kneeling down in front of her cousin, all her stateliness banished by secret exultation. 'You saw him, I know, Martha. You came back in the same train with him.'

'But not in the same carriage,' replied Martha, who had indeed avoided John on her return, as though he had been plague-stricken.

'Was he alone at the London station— quite alone?' questioned Mary, with kindling eyes. 'You say "yes," Patty, but you mumble the words in so odd a way that I vow I hardly believe you.'

Martha cowered over the fire in silence. Did Mary know anything? And if so, how much?

'You are late,' said John to her presently, when he joined them in the room; and his eyes rested coldly on the meek little figure, almost as if he disapproved of her being still in her cloak and bonnet. 'I thought you meant to return by the two o'clock train?'

'I—I was detained. It's — it's nearly dinner-time,' stammered Martha, and hurried away, fearful of further questioning.

'One would almost think you had an interest in Martha's returning early,' remarked Mary, looking straight into her brother's face.

'You are mistaken. Martha's movements have but a limited interest for me. *I* have never made her a confidante, nor employed her on clandestine errands,' retorted John.

'Which means that I have,' said Mary tranquilly. 'Union is strength, John. Why should you and I not make mutual confidences, with a view to mutual advantage?'

'You must demonstrate to me first the nature of the confidences which I could have to make,' replied her brother, his marble face more inscrutable than ever.

She kept her eyes fixed on him for a space, then saying, ' It will be your own fault if I am alienated,' relapsed into silence.

It was a few weeks later that Martha and John found themselves alone at breakfast. The circumstance was not an unusual one, for Mr. Hatherley of course was never present, and Mary just now had reached that stage of a sentimental grievance which results in incapacity for all the minor tasks of life.

The post-bag had arrived, and John, after sorting the letters, was engaged in reading his own. He had handed the *Times* to his cousin, not for her own perusal, but to cut and smooth for his, and if he thought of her at all, he probably supposed her to be taking the opportunity to glance at it. But Martha's mind, not intellectually inclined at the best of times, had no room in it at present for news of the Spanish marriages or any subjects of a kindred

nature. Her eyes were fixed on John. Ever
since the day of her exciting discovery, he
had possessed a kind of fascination for her.
Lately also, certain circumstances had happened which had the effect of increasing Miss
Freake's interest in him. His double existence as a bachelor in Marleyford, and a
married man in London; his unaltered
dignity and unruffled calm under the weight
of such a fact, lifted him in her simple mind
to an epic grandeur of audacity. She had
fallen into the habit of watching him, quite
unconscious of the annoyance it gave him and
the sullen dislike which she was thus creating
in his mind against her.

A thrill of absolute excitement ran through
her now on noticing that one of John's letters
seemed to cause him agitation. He changed
colour visibly on reading the first lines, and
turned hastily to the signature. That apparently did not afford him any satisfaction
either, for he frowned angrily. Martha, her
loving inquisitiveness fully roused, strained

her short-sighted eyes in a vain endeavour to guess the nature of the communication. The writing was small and cramped—so much she could make out, and something in its general air had a queer, distorted kind of likeness to Mary's hand. This circumstance, which poor Martha had good cause to remember later, struck her now but for a passing moment, as a mere imperfect coincidence.

Convinced that the writing was a woman's, she was not slow in attributing it to the mysterious lady in Linden-Grove Road ; and her imagination, always romantic, began to suggest a thousand possibilities. When John, rising at last, announced that he would have to go that day to London, and that he might not be back to dinner, Martha became more and more persuaded that some crisis had occurred in the clandestine establishment.

' If he would only tell me—trust to me ! I might be of some use !' she thought pathetically, her glance following his tall figure, and affectionately dwelling on his inscrutable face.

'Thank ye! thank ye !' said John brusquely, as Martha, ridiculously too short, stood on tip-toe in a futile endeavour to help him with his great-coat. He was cross, and the attention bored him, while she lovingly excused all things in him, including petulance to herself.

He started for the door ; then suddenly paused, and turned to address her.

'Martha, I hear Mr. Luscombe was here one day last week in my absence. Do you know why he came?' He asked the question with an air of great carelessness, but his eyes were watchful.

'Mr. Luscombe ? He spoke with your father,' murmured Martha, turning very red.

'Of course. But of what? Ah! I see you do not intend to enlighten me.' And John, with a displeased expression, walked away.

Mr. Luscombe was the family lawyer, and he had of late paid one or two visits to Hatherley House. And Martha, on her side, had been rather oftener than usual to London.

These two facts had reached John's knowledge and proved unwelcome. Her reserve did not tend to put him in a better humour; on the contrary, it increased the vague feeling of irritation against her that he had been conscious of for weeks.

John had hardly left the house, when Mary appeared. Her breakfast and letters were always taken up to her, and she did not generally come down until late. But on this occasion she had seemingly been only waiting for her brother's departure to descend. She was looking pale yet exultant, and her eyes were bright with excitement.

' Patty,' she began, with the charming grace that she displayed at times, and that her cousin always found irresistible, ' tell me, did John seem annoyed by anything this morning?'

Martha was fain to admit that he did : and by dint of further questioning, Mary elicited the fact that it was a letter which had caused it.

'Patty, I want you to do me a favour,' she said, later in the day.

'Anything you like, darling,' replied her fervid and incautious slave.

'I wonder if I can trust you,' continued Mary, contemplating her reflectively. 'You make dreadful blunders sometimes, Patty.'

Martha, oppressed by the consciousness of her stupidity, had nothing to say.

'I must risk it,' said Mary, lowering her voice confidentially. 'I want you to go to the post-office the day after to-morrow, and get a letter that will be lying there addressed to "X. Y. Z." You must bring it direct to me.'

Mary had expected eager compliance, and was surprised to see no sign of it, but to be met by silence. 'Well?' she exclaimed impatiently.

Martha's face presented a study of contending emotions. This was the second time that Mary had made a request to her which she found it difficult to grant. She feared, her secret knowledge rendering her imaginative, that some trap was being laid for John, and to that she could not be a party.

'This which you beg of me to do, is it anything unworthy?' she asked, shrinking from the question, even while she uttered it, because loth to hint at the shadow of evil in connection with Mary Hatherley.

That young lady became rather red, but also rather angry.

'You are so absurd of late,' she exclaimed. 'Of course it is nothing unworthy. Only a little piece of poetical justice; fun, in fact. I—that is—a friend of mine and myself, we wish to give my saintly brother a fright.'

Martha looked grave.

'You must tell me more.'

'To tell you would spoil the whole,' said Mary petulantly. 'If you don't go I shall send some one else, and then there is no knowing what mischief may ensue. Any stranger sent on such an errand would think that some important secret is concerned, and

might open the letter. He would talk : and
only imagine the effect of such talking in
Marleyford !'

Martha made no immediate reply. Mary's
words had for her a greater force than the
speaker could guess. She had not, it is true,
an idea of the nature of the letter, or of the
measure to which it could affect John; and on
the other hand, she dared not question. She
feared by interrogation to excite suspicion and
illuminate facts still wrapped up in darkness.

'You cannot refuse me such a little favour,
Patty,' began Mary once more, caressingly.
The coaxing tone went to her cousin's heart.
Still she could not yield at once. Mary en-
treated, repeating again and again that the
letter must be withdrawn, 'if not by Martha,
then by somebody else.'

'If I bring you the letter, what will you do
with it ?' asked the yielding woman.

'Tear it up,' answered Mary with a light
laugh, that yet was a little forced.

' You promise,' questioned Martha, looking at her earnestly.

' I promise,' replied the girl : though her glance flickered.

Martha sighed. But love and anxiety for those she loved combined to vanquish her ; and Mary, triumphant, finally extracted from her the promise that she would go.

The day came, and Miss Freake went; but no letter was forthcoming. Mary, much disappointed, insisted on her promise to go again at the end of another few days.

So one fine morning, when the air was balmy, although the trees were still leafless, and when crocuses and snowdrops had suddenly revealed themselves in all the gardens, Martha started off once more, the post-office her final destination. First she had many small errands of business and of charity to perform ; some bills to pay, some bedridden crones to visit. Blither than usual, the cloud of humble depression which generally clung around her gentle spirit a little lifted, she trotted from place to place. Perhaps it was the soft, lovely weather that made her feel so bright ; for Martha Freake was very sensitive to external impressions. Far more sensitive, indeed, than most people, looking carelessly at her crumpled little face under her dowdy bonnet, thought it worth while to guess. Poor simple, loving Martha !

At last she turned into the street where the post-office was ; presented herself before the clerk, and asked for a letter addressed ' X.Y.Z.' It was handed out to her. With a spasm of surprise, she recognised the handwriting of the address for John's. Hastily thrusting the mysterious missive into her pocket, she turned and found herself face to face with a quiet-looking stranger. What he had to say to her, and what happened next, the curious reader will learn in the following chapter.

CHAPTER III.

THE WILL.

PSTAIRS, in a warm, comfortable, remote room, where the bustle and stir of the household could not reach, Mr. Hatherley spent his days. They were monotonous drowsy days, saddened by weakness and the sense of an imminent end.

The brewer had never possessed many mental resources : never had been a reading man, or made his son's pretensions to culture.

Now, as the gloom of weakness and of age gathered round his spirit, he had but one occupation. That was, to go over and over again in memory the details of long-past business operations. His mind was very clear, but his vivid interest in present things as a rule had vanished. Generally silent, and a little morose, rather than patient and resigned, he would flash out at intervals into energy or anger. And his intelligence on these occasions was still so keen, his views so decided, his will so swift and strong, that the whole household shrank from rousing the slumbering lion. His restless irritability and proportional sharpness of insight, kept his children and servants on thorns, for the lightest word sufficed to annoy, and the faintest indication to enlighten him.

Late one afternoon he sat at his usual place by the fire, the landscape still dimly visible through the unshuttered windows. The reflection of the blaze on walls and furniture became ruddier by contrast with the shadows which it could only partially chase. The servant on bringing the lamp had been bidden to take it away again. Silently, almost humbly, he obeyed, for the day had been one of Mr. Hatherley's worst; and now he was supposed to have sunk into the semi-stupor which generally followed his outbursts of excitement. He had a rugged, stern, old face—the set face of a man who had known few, although strong, emotions, and responded to fewer ideas. But now on the sunken, cold lips a softer expression than usual dwelt. Once or twice the wrinkled hands trembled, and an open letter which they held rustled as in answer to some quiver of the aged frame.

' All in the dark, father ?' exclaimed Mary, entering suddenly. ' How careless of Jacobs !' And she rang the bell.

The old man did not seek to justify Jacobs, or to answer. He still seemed lost in thought. Mary glanced at him rather impatiently, and no quick instinct of love warned her of the subtle change in his air. Her mind was, as always, full of her own affairs. Earlier in the day she had almost decided to appeal to him for money; but his mood had been ungracious, and her courage failed.

When the lights were brought in, he roused

himself a little, and, lifting his eyes, fixed them on his daughter with a singular, wistful look, almost of tenderness. She was startled—even shivered with a vague awe. Never before had he so looked at her; and recalling the mystic change that sometimes precedes death, she wondered whether it were some prescience of his end which now filled her father's eyes with that strange regretfulness.

She laid her hand on his wrinkled, trembling fingers, generally so nerveless, and felt them close kindly, although feebly, round her own.

'You are like your mother to-night, my dear, it seems to me,' he said. 'Or perhaps it is only that I have been living all day in the past.'

'Can I do anything for you, father? Is there anything you want?' asked Mary, oppressed by the silence and by her own unwonted emotion. Her shallow nature could not long bear the strain of a painful feeling. She wished he would take those wan, solemn, regretful eyes from her face.

'I have thought of you a great deal to-day,' he resumed, the senile trembling of his lips increasing as the slow words came through them; 'of you and Will. I have been reading his last letter; that one in which he says he is about to marry. You remember?'

'Yes; you said it was certain to be a marriage to disgrace us,' said Mary jealously, for there had been scant love between herself and her younger brother, and she had no desire to see him reinstated in her father's favour.

'Ay,' answered Mr. Hatherley; 'I said so, I remember. But things seem different now. I should like him to be happier than he has been.'

'He does not deserve much happiness that I can see,' replied Mary, too angry now for tenderness.

'I have been unjust to him, and not generous to you, my dear. I was over-persuaded.'

'By John?' cried Mary, a sudden light breaking upon her.

'Yes,' he answered musingly. 'John is hard, but I thought him just, and I had faith in him until now.   Lately——'

He paused, and his head drooped again. Mary was livid with excitement at the thought of the danger she had barely escaped—nay, which perhaps still hung over her head. Should she tell that secret something she knew of her brother, or would silence be wiser?   Resentment and self-interest alike urged her to speak.

'Father, I have a thing to tell you—a secret of John's,' she said, grasping the old man's arm in the intensity of her eagerness.

He lifted his eyes to hers, but they had a wandering look which alarmed her.   Were the shades of death already obscuring his tardily-awakened conscience ?   Was he drifting away so fast that her touch could no longer detain, her voice no longer reach him? In a spasm of fear she fell on her knees beside him.

'I should like to reverse the will,' he murmured. 'But perhaps I have no time.'

The whispered, mournful words sickened Mary. What had he done? Was she to be left penniless? Springing up, she hastily collected pens, ink, and paper. 'Dictate!' she exclaimed. 'I can write, and you can sign it.'

Once again succeeded a moment of that terrifying silence, during which, breathless, she leant forward and peered into his face. But it was the slow gathering together of his enfeebled faculties that made the pause; for suddenly he roused himself, and in clear tones, with a steadfast look, began to dictate:

'February 10th, 184—. Besides the minor legacies mentioned in my latest will, I leave to my daughter Mary, and to my son William, £30,000 each for their own exclusive use and benefit. The remainder of my real and personal estate I leave in the manner already set forth.'

His voice ceased. Mary looked up. Before she could speak, he stretched out his hand towards the pen.

'Call Jacobs and Gregory as witnesses. Be quick, child! I think the sands are slipping fast.'

She flew to the bell, and its summons not being answered rapidly enough for her impatience, sped down the staircase calling 'Jacobs! Jacobs!' at the top of her voice.

'Quick!' she cried, when half a dozen startled servants came running. 'Jacobs, come! Somebody call Gregory. Your master wants two witnesses to his signature to a will.'

'A will? At the eleventh hour, as you may say, poor gentleman — what a freak!' commented Mrs. Hoare, the housekeeper, while she despatched an underling for Gregory, the gardener, and Jacobs followed his excited young mistress upstairs.

Mary, of course, was the first to gain the room, and then Jacobs heard her give a shrill cry of astonishment and dismay. On putting

in his questioning countenance, Jacobs found
Mr. Hatherley in his usual attitude by the
fire, Mary standing speechless in the middle
of the floor, and upon the hearth-rug, quietly
warming himself, imperturbably irreproach-
able, was—John!

The two servants, who had now come,
could not take in the full meaning of the
scene, for they felt that there was some
mystery, and remained staring, silent and
puzzled.

'What is the matter?' inquired John affably.

Jacobs looked at Gregory, and Gregory at
him ; after which, both directed glances at
their young mistress. But she seemed dumb-
founded, and vouchsafed not a word.

'Miss Mary said, sir, that we were wanted
to witness a will,' replied Jacobs respectfully.

'A will?' repeated John sharply. 'What
will ? My father's ? I think you are all
mad.'

Then Mary, beside herself, burst out: 'I
tell you the codicil was there . . . . on that

table . . . . a codicil destroying your frauds.
You have taken it. Give it back!'

Her words came out in gasps. She was
half-suffocated with an emotion which, in all
her decorous life, she had never felt or shown
before. At last she positively rushed at her
brother, as if to wrest the truth from him;
but he seized her by the wrists and held her
at arms'-length, his cold contemptuous eyes
scanning her face.

'You are disgracing yourself, Mary. You
are dreaming. Where is the codicil? Look
for it,' he concluded quietly.

Where was it indeed?

Mary turned imperiously to her father, but
even her anger shrank from questioning him;
for he was sitting back in his chair quite silent
and still, with a fascinated look of horror in
his eyes, and a trembling of his whole frame
inexpressibly painful to see. The scene was
evidently too much for his failing strength,
and it was more than likely that whatever he
knew he would not tell. On the floor was a

crumpled sheet of paper. Mary pounced upon it, but threw it away again the next moment, on finding that it was only William's letter. Her hungry eyes turned to the fire, but no trace of any consumed document was there; so again she faced her brother. He had never taken his gaze off her, and now spoke as calmly as before:

'You are convinced of your folly, I hope ? No ? Then I am tired of it, and I think the servants had better withdraw.'

Gregory and Jacobs took the hint, and vanished. Mary cast herself upon a sofa, sobbing. John stood by with a gloomy frown. All at once, across the stormful silence, Mr. Hatherley spoke. 'I wish,' he said, slowly and distinctly, 'to be left alone.'

Both his children started with a momentary sense of remorse. The quiet command so feebly yet so authoritatively spoken, falling into the midst of their sordid self-absorption, was like a voice from the tomb.

'Come to your room,' said John to his

sister, who had stayed her sobs and risen. 'I have to speak to you seriously, and we worry my father. You will ring for Hoare if you want her, sir ;' and John, after a keen, dissatisfied glance, crossed the room and bolted the door communicating with the servants' staircase.

Signing to Mary to follow him, he led the way to her bedroom, and closed the door. 'It is nearly dinner-time,' he began. 'Has it struck you as strange that Martha should still be out?'

Martha? The subject was so unexpected at that moment, that Mary absolutely started. 'I have had other things on my mind,' she replied sullenly.

' She did not return to lunch, and she will not be here to dinner,' said John. 'It seems you have heard nothing ?'

'Nothing at all; nobody has called to-day,' answered Mary slowly, looking at him with a growing feeling of disaster. She did not wish to ask what had happened; but he re-

mained silent, and she could not bear the
suspense.

'Where is Martha?'

'In gaol.'

Mary shrieked. The words were like a stab.
But even then it was the blow to herself of the
announcement which she felt most of all.

'Cruel! cruel!' she cried, and covered her
face with her hands.

'The cruelty belongs to the person who sent
her on a felonious errand,' retorted John. 'I
was amazed when I heard of it. Mr. Ormerod
called himself at the brewery about it, twice.
The first time I was out; and this and other
delays made it impossible to get her out on
bail to-day. But to-morrow, when she is
brought up for examination, I shall of course
do what I can for her, although I am myself
the prosecutor.'

Mary sat listening, half-stunned, to the cold,
commonplace words; commonplace in their
meaning, and as John uttered them, but tragic
in their significance to her. Two questions

kept recurring constantly to her, beating
against her brain like hammers. 'What would
happen to herself? and what to Ralph?'

'Do you wish Martha to remain under this
charge?' he asked.

'I?' she repeatedly faintly.

'She has only been your tool: and, as I
believe, your innocent tool,' continued John.
'If I state this conviction before the magistrates to-morrow, she will be discharged.'

Mary wrung her hands. All the consequences
to herself were beginning to dawn upon her.

'I need not point out that disgrace will fall
on you, even though you are not arrested as
Ralph Mercer's accomplice,' he pursued unre-
lentingly. But if Mary had not brains she had
some courage, and his tone stung her to revolt.

'You are trying to frighten me with your
talk of felony and punishment, John. But
after all, what the letter said was perfectly
true. You have a clandestine establishment,
and you wish to keep it a secret.'

'That is quite true. But the mista   you

and Ralph made was in menacing me, supposing that I would pay a large price for the
secret to be kept.' Mary started. This was a
new aspect of the question.

'To my wife, herself (for the lady in Linden-
Grove Road is my wife), nobody could make
any objection. But I will not conceal from
you that there are circumstances connected
with her which might render my father angry
at the marriage——'

'And leave you out of his will,' interrupted
Mary, with scorn.

'Precisely.'

His coolness exasperated her. Her eyes
flashed, and she was about to make some
angry observation when he raised his hand to
impose silence.

'Let us talk frankly, Mary. If I am in your
power to a degree of which, observe, you are
ignorant, *you* are in *my* power to an extent of
which I am fully aware. Martha, poor soul,
between bewilderment and loyalty, said very
little to-day, and nothing that could compro-

mise you. But she evidently counts upon
you to release her from her present position,
and it is impossible to say how long her
silence may last when she finds herself mistaken. Her story, to the prejudiced ears of
Marleyford — prejudiced in our favour,' said
John, with an air of sardonic satisfaction—
'will probably at first strike everybody as
wildly improbable, but its ultimate acceptance
will largely depend upon me. If I state my
conviction that my cousin was my sister's
cat's-paw, I fancy our kind neighbours and
friends will, one and all, accept the succulent
morsel of scandal whole. Martha will be
pitied as a victim and exalted as a martyr ;
shall bring my wife, her existence no longer
a secret, in triumph home ; while you, my
dear—well! I leave you to imagine the figure,
more novel than edifying, that you will cut.'

Mary was speechless with dismay and rage.
In the last few minutes she had lived through
a decade of mental experience. She saw her
respectability in men's eyes—that elaborate

fabric built up of family tradition and personal
pride—threatened to its foundations ; she was
frightened for her lover, frightened for herself,
a little remorseful about Martha ; and aghast,
to the point of pain, at the unexpected revelation of her brother's true character.

'I—I declare I do not know you !' she
exclaimed.

'You do not know me because this is the
first time in our lives that the clash of
antagonistic interests has brought out the
essential difference between us. If you will
have confidence in me—good. If not, Mary,
you will have nobody but yourself to blame
for anything unpleasant that may happen to
you.'

Her nerves irritated by his stern composure,
his calm superiority, Mary again sought refuge
in tears. He let her sob for a little while.

'Now, Mary, for the question of the money.
I have just detected you in the attempt to
obtain a codicil by undue influence.'

'My father volunteered to make it,' she

flashed out, restored to some momentary energy.

' The proof ? Let me tell you that a codicil in your own favour and *your own handwriting*, would look very suspicious in the eyes of the law. And why do you object to the original will ?'

' For aught I know I am disinherited,' she said, falling into the trap laid for her, and betraying her real ignorance of her father's intentions.

John indulged in a smile of quiet triumph ; and as he had learnt all he needed to know, he was gratified at this moment to hear the clash of the gong.

' Seven o'clock, I declare! Come, Mary, dry your eyes, and be reasonable. You will certainly make ducks and drakes of any money which is left you ; but at the same time, if it be any comfort to you to know that you will not starve, of that I can assure yon. You are in a hole, and so is Ralph, for that affair of the letter is criminal ; but if I am pleased

with you, I will stand your friend. And we
will get Martha off also—call her insane,
perhaps.'

Cowed afresh by this reiteration of the
danger hanging over her, Mary rose, sulkily
but obediently, and accompanied her brother
downstairs. There the respectful Jacobs was
waiting for them, and the dinner began in its
usual form.

But it was not destined to be thus concluded. All at once the silent brother and
sister were startled by the sound of a heavy
fall in the room above, which was Mr. Hatherley's sitting-room. They looked at one
another with questioning eyes, and John half
rose from his seat, listening.

At this moment in rushed Mrs. Hoare, pale
and scared.

'Oh, sir! the master! . . . he is lying
insensible! . . . I think he is dead.'

When the son and daughter reached their
father's side, they found him lost to all consciousness, but still breathing. The doctor,

summoned in haste, pronounced the attack to
be a fresh seizure, and declared his conviction
that it was destined to be the last ; which
sent the whole house into a commotion.

In point of fact, the old man never rallied,
and, just when the dawn was breaking, he
went. John was calm, but grave and attentive ; Mary, shattered with fatigue, and
worn out by a quick succession of emotions,
quite subdued.

' Now, don't take on, my dear,' said Mrs.
Hoare, forgetting something of her acquired
respect in her native motherliness. ' What is
it you say? If he had only spoken again?
Well, well, the ways of Providence are
mysterious. And it is quite certain the poor
gentleman loved you ; and if he had been
unjust, his intention was likely to remedy it—
or I should not have found him standing
where I did,' concluded the good woman,
smoothing her apron with a casual air.

' What do you mean?' asked Mary, raising
her tear-stained face.

'You heard the fall? Yes. Well, I had gone into the room that instant. Poor master, he was standing by his writing-table, with his hand on the very drawer from which Mr. John has just carried a bundle of documents into his own room. He turned as I came in, and said, "Mrs. Hoare," he says, " later this evening, when Jacobs is free——" Then he stopped. " Yes, sir," says I, thinking he had only just stopped to reflect, may be. But he stood like a statue—his hand just raised. Miss, it was awful. It was as if he was listening to a distant voice. Then all at once his poor face was drawn, he gave a little gasp, and before I could catch him he had fallen in a heap upon the floor. And, Miss Mary, he never spoke again.'

This story of Mrs. Hoare's preoccupied Mary. She, as well as the housekeeper, had seen John remove a bundle of papers from a drawer of his father's writing-table and take them to his own room. Was the codicil among these? If so, John's first care would

of course be to destroy it. Mary knew that
an unsigned codicil was not of much legal
value, but a thought, sharpened by resentment, suggested to her that it might be of
some use in enabling her to dispute her
father's will, should that prove, as she feared,
too flagrantly unjust. What was her father
doing at the writing-table when Mrs. Hoare
found him there? In the state of inertness
and weakness in which he was, he must have
had some strong motive to impel him to the
exertion of creeping across the room. Perhaps
he had had possession of the codicil all the
time, and had taken advantage of being alone
to conceal it, intending to get the servants to
witness it later.

All at once it flashed across Mary's mind
that this writing-table of her father's possessed
a curious secret drawer. Ralph Mercer had
told her of it. He had heard of it from
William Hatherley, who, coming unexpectedly
once into his father's study, had caught sight
of it ere the old man had hastily and furtively

closed it. William confessed to having taken an occasion to look for it, but in spite of many shakings and rappings he had been completely baffled. And the one chance which enabled him to make his search had never repeated itself. William, wisely distrustful of his brother, had carefully kept from him all knowledge of his discovery, although to his 'chum,' Ralph, he had been frank. Mary, recalling all this, asked herself: 'Could the codicil be there?' She longed to find it, unable to believe that it would not be of some use.

John had gone out in the course of the morning about the necessary arrangements, and except for the servants she was alone in the house. The opportunity was too good to be lost, and she went to the rooms where her father had spent his last sad and silent months. A little shudder of awe came over her as she glanced at the fireless hearth, the empty armchair, at all the familiar unchanged objects whose special use was gone. With a superstitious shrinking she softly closed the door, left ajar, of the darkened bedroom, where lay the still presence so full of rebuke in its unconscious majesty; and then she began her search.

But it was as fruitless now for her, as it had ever been for William : she could not hit upon the secret of the drawer. Such papers as she found she scanned eagerly, but there were none of any importance : John had taken care of that. Feeling herself foiled, Mary leant her face upon her hands and began to weep silently. She was thoroughly exhausted, and felt dreadfully sorry for herself. She recalled the touch of new kindness towards her in her father's tone and manner the day before, and sobbed bitterly. Nobody was ever so lonely as she : even Martha was not there to comfort her : she had been taken into custody on suspicion of having written the threatening letter.

Selfishly confiding in John's assurance that Martha could be ' got off somehow,' Mary had

dismissed as much as possible from her mind
the thought of Miss Freake's present position.
Now it recurred to her, and with it a sense of
her own baseness. She was just in one of
those moods when to think one's self vile seems
equal to a return to virtue. Crossness with
the world produced in Mary an inclina-
tion to defy it. It would be grand of her,
and it would startle Marleyford, if she were
publicly to proclaim Martha's innocence and
her own guilt. She began to rehearse the
scene in her mind. She would appear before
the magistrates, looking very interesting in
her mourning, and in clear tones she would
state the truth. She could not be punished
very severely after that ; John would be de-
frauded of his intention of putting her down ;
Mrs. Hoare's story would help her in threatening to dispute the will. John would have to
compound for a large sum of money ; and she
—well, she and Ralph would marry, and take
the grateful Martha home to live with them.
The picture was charming. It quite cheered

her, and she rose to her feet with a sense of heroism.

But a thought intervened. Had not John said that Martha would be brought up again before the magistrates this very morning? In that case the time for action was *now*. This check, like a brigand with a cocked pistol on a lonely road, brought Mary up rather suddenly. She still felt inspired, only inspired for some less definite epoch — perhaps to-morrow or next day. While she hesitated and began to get rather ill-tempered, Jacobs knocked at the door. The diversion was a relief. 'Come in,' she said.

'Mr. Russell is in the library, Miss Mary. He wishes to know if he can do anything for you.'

'I will see him,' said Mary : and, as well as the lowered blinds would allow, she scanned herself in the glass to see if her tears had disfigured her. She did not care for Walter Russell ; but it was gratifying to know that he was devoted to her, more espe-

cially as everybody admired him, and wondered
why she did not prefer him to Ralph Mercer.
As she went downstairs it occurred to her
that perhaps she might make her first confession about Martha to him. It would be a
pretty scene—she remorseful, more sinned
against than sinning; he touched and tender
and very indulgent. He would smooth her
after-path, and stand between her and blame.

Paler than usual, with a graver but a
gentler manner and an air of lovely languor,
she entered the library and responded to Mr.
Russell's moved and eager greeting. Her
stateliness always impressed him, and now
that it was informed with this new gracious-
ness he found it irresistible.

'I fear you are very sad,' he said kindly,
and held her hand. Mary sighed. She had
a retrospective vision of herself as she had
been ten minutes previously in her father's
room, and felt that she was indeed very, very
sad.

'I am glad you came. I was upstairs,' she

murmured ; and Walter, who understood her, pressed her hand sympathizingly.

'You are well?' said Mary, looking at him with a keener appreciation than usual of his refined and intelligent air. 'And your little cousin, Sir Charles's son, how is he?'

'He is, I fear, dying,' replied Walter gravely.

'Dying?' Mary was startled. If the boy died, Walter would be heir-presumptive to a baronetcy. Her opinion of him rose considerably.

'I am afraid there is very little chance for the poor child; but I did not come here to talk of my own affairs,' he said. 'I want to know, Miss Hatherley, if I can be of any service to you. I have been so shocked to hear, not only of your loss, but of this terrible business of Miss Freake's. Surely there must be some mistake?'

Mary's heart seemed to stand still. Now was her opportunity; now or never. She felt that her next words would seal her fate, as a soul with some possibility of redemption, or as the basest of liars.

There are these unchronicled crises in life that count for more than death or ruin. Mary Hatherley felt herself in the grip of a grim reality. The act of justice which, dressed in fantastic guise, had seemed easy of accomplishment an instant before, now stared at her with a terrible earnestness out of Mr. Russell's honest eyes. Never until this moment had she realized her folly, or felt that it was irrevocable. With a sob of impotent anger against herself and everybody, that admirably simulated pain, she bowed her head upon her arms and gave up truth for ever.

CHAPTER IV.

MARTHA'S SHAME.

HEN John Hatherley rode into the town, the morning after his father's death, he was the object of general and respectful sympathy. Two such events as Martha Freake's arrest and Mr. Hatherley's death, following immediately one upon the other, had not happened in Marleyford for a long time. The little town really felt as if i had pressure on the brain. How Martha was looking, what doing, saying, thinking behind her prison walls—how the Hatherleys were behaving inside their darkened house: such were the two subjects full of delightful mys-

tery. John, in his new character of master
and chief mourner, became most interesting ;
and wherever he stopped, on his way to the
magistrates' room, words of condolence greeted
him.

Fresh excitement was presently caused by
the rumble of a stately vehicle up the High
Street, and its instant recognition as the
Hatherley carriage, as it drew up at the court.
Who was inside it? Could it be Miss
Hatherley? Then followed a thrill of commotion as its occupant was recognised for Martha
Freake. John, looking sad but admirable,
hurried forward to help his cousin out, and
while the bystanders are struck dumb at his
goodness, Martha, thickly veiled and visibly
trembling, shuffles along and disappears.

When John looked at her, even he was
shocked at the change which twenty-four hours
had made. Not so much agitated, humiliated,
bewildered was she, as simply scared out of all
possibility of thought. She mechanically did
as she was told ; sat down in the chair pointed

out to her; answered all the questions addressed to her ; but not frankly and fearlessly
as the consciousness of her innocence should
have made her so do.   Rather did she seem
held back from replying by some unseen terror.
And it would have been touching to mark,
had anybody been there capable of marking, or
in the secret, how little the thought of betraying Mary Hatherley occurred to her.

Of course the magistrates, of whom Mr.
Ormerod was one, were very kind and consi-
derate to her.   This they would have been in
any case, out of respect for Martha's position
as well as for that of the Hatherleys.   But the
poor little woman had been so familiar a figure
to them for years; they had felt, quite unconsciously, so much reverence for her simple
goodness, that the sight of her there, and the
necessity of investigating the charge against
her, were things exquisitely painful.

Have you nothing to say in your own defence, Miss Freake ?' asked Mr. Ormerod,
when the case had been fully gone into, and

John had related the circumstances attendant upon his receipt of the threatening letter, and the steps he had taken to trace the writer of it.

She glanced round with a hunted look for a moment, almost as if fearing that the question might be a trap; then hung her head and murmured :

'I was told to go and fetch the letter.'

'By whom ?'

She was silent.

'Were you ignorant of its contents ?'

'Yes.'

'Were you positively not aware that the letter, to which it was a reply, was written with a view of extorting money ?'

'I was not aware of that.'

'Then you mean us to understand that the threatening letter was not written by you ?'

'Yes.'

'Did you suspect its true author ?'

Martha made a nervous movement with her hands.

'I knew nothing about it; nothing,' she said, her voice trembling with distress.

'But, Miss Freake,' expostulated Mr. Ormerod, 'cannot you understand that by persisting in this vague denial, not stating why you should have gone to the post-office for the letter, or who sent you, you place us in a most perplexing and painful position? Either you are guilty, or you are not guilty. If you will not speak, and clearly, we have no choice but to commit you for trial.'

She became violently agitated; her whole fragile frame shook.

'I will speak,' she cried wildly, 'but not here, not now. It is all a mistake; you must see that. Let me go home, I pray you, to Mary. I am not guilty; I have never done wrong, and I cannot bear this. I want to be with Mary Hatherley.'

Her one thought was to escape from the horrible publicity and the cruel strangeness of her present position. Once back in the old home, among the familiar faces of those who knew and, as she, poor soul, thought, loved her, it seemed to her impossible but that this appalling nightmare should pass away. The very walls must bear testimony for her there, where she had lived, from whence she had gone forth on missions of charity, and whither she had returned in joy and thankfulness when the good day's work was done.

'I must bind you over in two sureties to appear for trial at the Assizes, Miss Freake,' resumed Mr. Ormerod reluctantly.

'Then I need not go back to prison,' exclaimed Martha, seizing upon this idea.

'Not if you can find the sureties.'

'I will be one,' interposed John Hatherley.

'And I the other,' added the Rector, Mr. Stratton, who was present.

Martha was released. Her manner grew more natural immediately, like that of a lost child that has suddenly caught sight of its mother amid a group of questioning, strange faces. But she was not to be taken back to Mary. John had arranged that, in a few rapid words with Mr. Stratton. He put her into the carriage, and bid her wait. Then he returned to the Justice-room, where the gentlemen were talking.

'One is always unwilling to believe such charges against a person of position,' the Rector was saying. 'I do not know what to think of her manner. Can she have been made a tool of?'

'That is precisely what I have been asking myself,' interposed John, with his usual air of grave candour. 'I am unwilling, except indeed on the supposition of insanity, to believe my poor cousin capable of such an act. But then come the questions: Who has played upon her credulous good-nature? and who can so influence her as to ensure her silence? It is preposterous to think that she would willingly sacrifice herself to the extent of taking upon her own shoulders the guilt of another.'

'Can there be a man in the matter? You understand me: a—an *affaire de cœur?*' suggested Mr. Ormerod profoundly.

A little stir of amusement greeted the words; even John smiled.

'I do not think Martha loves anybody but Mary and myself,' he replied.

'Then I give it up,' said Mr. Ormerod. As did the others. For John, as the prosecutor, could clearly not be the instigator; and as for his sister, like Cæsar's wife, she was above suspicion.

'This is altogether so very distressing a business, especially at this moment, that it is a relief to think my cousin will be with you and Mrs. Stratton,' said John as he walked with the Rector back to the carriage. 'You must let me know in confidence anything that she may say. But I do fear her mind is unhinged.'

The Rector promised his best services, being indeed only too gratified to think that he was obliging John Hatherley.

'You must be overwhelmed with painful business of one sort and another, Mr. John. Your father's death; and now this!'

' The worst times have an end,' said John.

Martha, on finding herself at the Rectory, sank into a mournful silence. She gently answered all observations made to her, but only volunteered one request: which was to beg that Mary might be sent for. The fussy, ostentatious benevolence of Mr. Stratton towards her, and the unconcealed curiosity of his wife, repelled her confidence. They were a thousand miles from suspecting this, of course. They thought, indeed, worthy people, that they were behaving with admirable kindness and tact.

They could not know that, abruptly wrenched from her old associations, she was divorced from the greater part of herself. Of her real, gentle personality nothing asserted itself with any vividness in these days, but one intolerable sense of tragic loss and shame. And this feeling was itself so bound up with her old life and all its affections that she remained strangely indifferent to the sympathy or possible blame of those outside her house. It was of this she thought perpetually; of the work that she had done in it; of her little room bright with flowers and birds; of the servants who had waited on her so willingly. Above all, she thought of Mary. To see *her* was her one great longing. With Mary's arm round her, with Mary's eyes looking forgiveness for her confession, she would speak. But in this harsh world of strangers where she drew her breath in pain, to lift up her voice in shrill self-justification was to her impossible. She felt too crushed, too bewildered. She was, in fact, concentrated almost to the verge of insanity, and they simply thought her sullen.

Mary Hatherley little guessed how well she had been served by her determination not to bring her victim home. She had shrunk from the thought of meeting her, in the selfishness of her weak, unworthy nature. John had pointed out to her the danger of Martha's speaking, but even this consideration was not strong enough to overcome her reluctance. If Martha did speak, she and John could deny; but of that they both knew there was little fear : Martha Freake would never betray Mary.

Under the eyes of her victim she could not keep up the farce of her own innocence. Martha's presence and tears would distress her; and she would be weak (she was within an ace of thinking *generous!*) enough to blurt out everything. And that would be very foolish ; needless also, for John would be sure to arrange matters and get Martha off scot-free. And borne up by this persuasion, in her pallor, her languor and her mourning, Mary presented a very interesting and a genuinely sad appearance to the few visitors admitted to Hatherley House on the days succeeding her father's death.

To Martha she wrote, saying that as soon as the funeral was over, she would visit her. Buoyed up by this hope, the patient woman waited.

Marleyford, now that Miss Freake was committed for trial, turned its interest from her to Mr. Hatherley's will. How he would leave his property; whether the distant reprobate, his son William, would be well remembered by him; what Mary's share of the family wealth might be; and what measure of responsibility would devolve upon John.

After the funeral, when Mr. Luscombe, the family lawyer, found only an old will was produced, he looked greatly surprised.

'Your father made a second will, about a month since,' he said curtly. Only Mary and John and the servants were present ; for the funeral guests had left, and of distant relatives, beyond Ralph Mercer and Martha Freake, the Hatherleys had none.

'A second will ?' repeated John. 'I have found none but this. Perhaps he deposited the second will with you ?'

'If he had, I should have brought it with me,' retorted Mr. Luscombe, irritated at the superfluous suggestion. 'As you must well know, he had a mania for keeping possession of his own papers.'

'Quite so,' assented John. 'And I found

this will in the private bureau, with other important documents. I am sure the second will would have been there had he preserved it ; but he probably destroyed it.'

Mr. Luscombe looked strangely unassentient, even a little suspicious. ' Why should he destroy it ?'

John slightly shrugged his shoulders. ' He appears to have been in several minds about his property, just before the end. The very evening of his death, Mary found him drawing up a third will — which *he certainly* destroyed.'

' Certainly ?'

' No doubt. When we were summoned by the noise of his fall, I noticed that the bureau, near which he was standing, was open, and in . the grate were several half-consumed papers.'

' Humph !' Mr. Luscombe glanced at Mary, but she sat like a graven image in her deep mourning, her face framed with its golden hair. The colour had indeed flushed once or twice into her cheeks at some of

John's answers. But no other sign of protest broke from her, for her brother's glacial glance held her terror-stricken and mute. The lawyer pondered for a few moments; then, with the gesture of a man who dismisses a subject of perplexity from his mind, he turned to the will lying before him on the table, and began to read it aloud. It was brief, but astounding, and may be summarily described by saying that with the exception of a few legacies to servants and others, John was left sole legatee. Mary and William were disinherited.

For one moment after the lawyer's tones ceased, Mary sat quite silent. When she found voice at last, it was only to utter a half-stifled cry of rage. She was so deadly pale that they thought her on the verge of fainting, and hurried towards her in alarm. John himself approached her and laid his hand upon her arm.

At the touch she shrank away, and burst into one of her storms of **rage**, her words coming so fast as almost to choke her voice.

She would dispute the will, she cried ; she would write to Jamaica, and bring William home. *These* were never her father's intentions. The servants could testify to so much. And when she told all she knew, the world would believe her.

'Dear ! dear ! dear !' exclaimed Mr. Luscombe, shaking his head and looking very much distressed. He had old-fashioned notions of the conduct becoming in young ladies, and was dreadfully shocked to see the beautiful Miss Hatherley behave like a Mænad.

Mary's exclamations subsided at length into angry sobs. John's smooth voice then broke the silence.

'I am not surprised that my sister should be disappointed. I can only hope that when her present excitement has calmed down, she will understand how little intention I have of behaving otherwise than generously.' Mary lifted her face from her handkerchief, met her brother's eyes, and buried it again. 'I think,' resumed John, again addressing the lawyer, 'that my poor father probably did half repent himself at odd moments of his harshness. Perhaps the second will you mention was more favourable to my brother and sister?'

'Not a whit,' answered Mr. Luscombe briskly.

John raised his eyebrows. 'My father must have destroyed it.'

The lawyer advised its being looked for; and a thorough search was instigated. It lasted all that day and the next, but ended without success. Mary meanwhile had ample time for reflection. John was careful to remind her constantly in a thousand subtle ways how completely she was in his power; and the dominion over her of his superior calmness increased with every hour. Mr. Luscombe—very suspicious at last about the wills, although long unwilling to be so—tried to elicit some light from her, but failed. She even disavowed the words which had fallen from her in her rage. The servants, grateful for their legacies and anxious to conciliate the heir, were equally discreet ; Mr. Luscombe, although his secret thoughts were many, and he asked John a few questions which surprised him, could but accept the facts as they stood.

Poor William Hatherley blustered a little from Jamaica when the news reached him; but having no money and no credit, he could not come over : and finally, on John's promising to supply his wants in the present and to look after his wife and children should he die, he followed the general example and sank into quiescence.

The only will found was, in consequence, proved : and one or two of its clauses as well as its general disposition gave Marleyford something to talk about. To this subject we will return later : suffice it to say for the present that John covered himself with fresh glory by the munificence of his conduct towards his brother and sister ; and everybody

was enraptured at the sweetness of Miss
Hatherley in accepting her disinheritance and
showing no resentment.

We must now go back to Martha Freake,
who for the days before Mr. Hatherley's
funeral, and for some weary ones after it, sat
counting the hours for her meeting with Mary.
Twice had the visit been promised, then de-
ferred. But at last Mary came.

They fell weeping into one another's arms.
All the pent-up anguish and bewildered, un-
answered questioning of days found vent in
the passionate outburst of sobs with which
Martha clung to her cousin. And there was
comfort for her in the responsive emotion
that shook Mary's frame. Ah! she was not
heartless ; she would speak, and this long
nightmare would dissolve for ever.

'Oh Patty, I am so unhappy !' sobbed
Mary, finding words.

Martha's tender heart overflowed at this
announcement. She noted with loving compassion her darling's altered air ; she stroked

her golden curls, and held her hands. Never doubting but that Mary's sorrow was all for her, she was filled with remorse and gratitude.

'You have heard?' said Miss Hatherley at last, disengaging herself from these caresses, and lifting her lovely eyes, full of the languor of regret, to the poor, deprecating face.

'Heard?' Martha had heard many new things of late. The world seemed topsy-turvy.

'How shamefully I have been treated : cut off with a shilling,' added Mary, in indignant explanation.

Martha stepped backwards. It was very selfish of her, of course; but she had really been thinking of herself, of her own trouble.

'What enrages me the more is that I know it is John's doing,' continued Mary, and went off into a confused, fretful monologue. Martha listened like one in a dream. She had not expected this. Not all the experiences of the past days had affected her like this discovery f Mary's callousness.

' And what are you going to do for me ?'
she abruptly asked, cutting short the string of
lamentations. Mary looked up quite startled;
the tone of the question was so new from
those lips. In Martha's eyes was a strange
sternness, and the other shrank before it.

' You will not betray me?' she faltered.

' Betray you?' Martha echoed the words
bitterly. ' You seem to forget that it is I
who am betrayed.'

Mary broke out into protest. How could
she say such things, or think them ? Of
course everything would come right in the
end. John had promised all that : only
Martha must have patience. As for the
charge, it was preposterous ; as all the world
saw. But it must not transpire that she,
Mary, had any knowledge of the letter. That
would make too dreadful a sensation in
Marleyford. What would the Ormerods think
— and Walter Russell — and everybody ?
Martha had always been good-natured; surely
she was not going to change in the face of

such a crisis? Mary's voice rose as she concluded. But Martha sat very quiet, very pale, but unshaken.

'Justice must be done to me,' she said. 'I have been silent because I believed in your honour. Now that it has failed me, I shall speak.'

'You seem quite to overlook the fact that nobody will believe you.'

The cruel words, wrung from Mary by the sheer spitefulness of abject fear, had hardly been uttered before she repented them. For Martha rose trembling in every limb, dumb, stricken to the heart, but with a glance so full of mournful majesty and of pitying scorn, that it was like an avenging angel's: and Mary's mean soul cowered beneath it.

With a convulsive sob she actually fell on her knees and clutched her cousin's hand.

'Oh Patty, dear Patty! have pity on me! Do not betray me. I shall be ruined. I shall have to leave Marleyford, and John will make my conduct an excuse not to give me a penny. Everybody will shun me. Even Ralph will not marry me then, perhaps. I shall starve. I shall be driven to despair— perhaps to suicide—I——'

'And I?' interrupted Martha. 'Have I no right to happiness and consideration, and the respect of my fellow-men? Is scorn less cutting, ruin less ruinous, shame less shame- ful, because the spirit stricken is mine, not yours? Shall I not suffer from outrage and privation and want? May I not be driven to suicide? Will the path be easier to tread for my feet than for your own?'

Mary sat silent, startled at the tragic ring of the words, but pettishly resentful of their unexpected eloquence. Martha again spoke.

'You have not answered me. Why am I to sacrifice my fair fame to yours?'

At the unconscious irony of the question, Mary took refuge in tears. Life had become an inextricable web of cross-purposes.

'You are so high-flown, and exaggerated, and—and unkind,' she sobbed sullenly. 'Who w—wants you to sacrifice your fame? Such a ridiculous expression! When I have told you that—that John will get you off the charge.'

'By some lie,' commented Martha, rendered wonderfully clear-sighted of late.

'You are so altered,' wailed Mary, wincing a little. 'I *never* thought you would object to save me—only just to keep silent and let matters take their course. You used to love me. I think now you must only want to disgrace me.'

'It is myself I want to save from disgrace, child,' answered Martha, with a sudden change of tone. Then to Mary's amazement—not unmixed, sooth to say, with some secret terror —she took her flushed, tearful face between her hands and turned it towards the light. Mary blanched under the glance that travelled slowly over her features.

'Pretty, golden-haired thing! Pretty,

shallow, flimsy piece of human nature !' exclaimed Martha at last. 'Perhaps you are
right after all, and disgrace would be absurdly
heavy for you. Well, you can go. We have
seen the last of one another ; the last in any
real sense.'

'And what are you going to do?' inquired
Mary.

'I shall defend myself.'

'It will be too late.'

'Perhaps so, for the world's verdict. But
that is a small matter. What is the world
now to me ?'

Martha sat down by the table as she
spoke, and laid her face upon her crossed
arms. The waters of bitterness were closing
over her soul. Mary crept to the door, opened
it softly, and found herself with a sense of relief in the passage.

Mrs. Stratton hurried forward obsequiously ;
the children came up with smiles and glances
of shy admiration for the beautiful Miss
Hatherley. In that atmosphere of flattery

Mary regained her usual self-complacency ; and the closed door between herself and Martha shut out also the consciousness of her crime. For moral sense with her meant only the approval of the world.

CHAPTER V.

'DEAF AND DUMB.'

AS the time for Martha Freake's trial drew near, public opinion became on the whole unfavourable to her.

'Guilty, no doubt,' said Marleyford, almost ashamed of its first compassion. 'She never was really *anybody*, poor thing, and the luxury of her life at the Hatherleys' must have demoralized her.'

When the eventful day dawned at last, the court was crowded to suffocation; the interest was intense, and had extended itself to the county town. It was generally known that

the defence was to be largely based on the plea
of insanity; and John had talked so much
about his cousin's remarkable eccentricity, that
the more obliging or the more ingenuous
spirits among his acquaintances had recalled
several odd traits in Miss Freake's character,
and declared themselves to have been much
struck with them at the time.

With all this it may be imagined what
curiosity was felt to see how Martha would
look at her trial. And her appearance sur-
passed expectation. She was worn to a
shadow; deadly pale, but for a settled flush on
each cheek; and her eyes, painfully bright, had
one fixed, startled stare. When asked to plead,
she said:

' Not guilty.'

Inspector Roberts stated that on receipt of
information furnished him by Mr. John
Hatherley, he had gone to the Marleyford post-
office, and had there found the prisoner. She
was asking for a letter addressed to ' X.Y.Z.'
She appeared more bewildered than frightened

when he arrested her, but had only said, ' You
will see it is all a mistake.'

John Hatherley next appeared. He looked
very handsome, very grave and dignified, with
an air of becoming concern; and he gave his
evidence, as the papers all said, ' with evident
reluctance.'

One morning he had received by post a
communication in a disguised hand, threatening him vaguely with exposure of his private
affairs, his ' secrets,' as the letter put it, unless
by a certain day (named) an answer, contain-
ing £50, was sent to Marleyford post-office
addressed to the initials ' X.Y.Z.' Scenting a
conspiracy, he had placed the matter in the
hands of the police.

The examination of the counsel for the
prosecution elicited from him three special
facts, of which the connection was not immediately visible. These were, first, that he
suspected nobody in particular of the author-
ship of the threatening letter; secondly, that
Martha Freake had superintended the establish-

ment at Hatherley House and dispensed the
housekeeping moneys ; thirdly, that a certain
bill of £50 to a builder had never been
paid.

Martha's face showed some slight glimmer
of indefinable emotion; and her counsel, Mr.
Wharton, made a movement of surprise. It
was his turn now to cross-examine, and he
rose. After one or two apparently un-
important questions, he asked in a brisker
tone :

'Then, do you positively assert, Mr. John
Hatherley, that you suspected no person at all
as the writer of the letter ?'

' I positively assert it.'

' You have no knowledge of any spiteful
persons, who may bear a grudge against you,
and——'

Of course the counsel for the prosecution in-
terfered at this point, and the Judge ruled that
the question was not a fair one. Whereupon
Mr. Wharton, with a shrug of his shoulders,
fell back upon those generalities which are

probably good as evidence to the legal mind,
but which to the uninitiated appear so hopelessly vague.

' Then it absolutely never occurred to you
that the person to present herself at the post-
office would be the prisoner ?'

' It never occurred to me.'

' You have said that the prisoner had for
fifteen years lived in your father's family, and
superintended the household. Also that a
great deal of money passed through her hands.
Did she not always render an accurate account
of the sums expended ?'

' Yes,' replied John. Then, after a slight
pause, he added ' generally.'

He spoke the word quite quietly, apparently
without obvious intention. Perhaps it was
only that barely-perceptible previous pause
which made it sound sinister; but as a matter
of fact it had a very bad effect.

The wiseacres among the audience shook
their heads, and the prisoner nervously clutched
the iron bar in front of her. She began to

tremble all over with uncontrollable agitation, looking, as many people whisperingly asserted at that moment, ' really guilty.'

' What do you mean by "generally"?' asked the counsel sharply.

' I mean almost always,' replied John.

' I must trouble you to be more explicit. Did the prisoner at any time not render such account to you ?'

' You have just heard that on one occasion she did not.'

' I wish to hear it again.'

Whereupon John, under pressure of further interrogation, related how he had owed £50 to one Smithson, a builder ; how the man had asked to be paid in money and not by cheque ; how John, driving with his sister and Miss Freake that day into town, had stopped at the bank and drawn £100 in notes. He kept £50 himself, and had given the other £50 into Miss Freake's hands, requesting her, as he was himself just leaving by train for London, to call round and pay Smithson his account. Hearing no more from the builder, he concluded that this had been done.

' When was this ?'

' Shortly before my father's death. Not many days, I think, before I received the threatening letter.'

' When did you discover that the bill had not been paid ?'

' Only yesterday,' replied the witness. ' To my surprise, Mr. Smithson stopped me in the street with a renewed request for the money.'

This story created great excitement. Its significance was borne in gradually upon the audience as each fresh answer to the keen questions of the cross-examining counsel only established John's testimony the more firmly. Young Mr. Hatherley's manner was quite that of a man who feels fully all his responsibilities.

The missing £50, lost or otherwise disposed of by Martha, supplied that motive for the anonymous letter, which even the most eager of her non-partizans had hitherto felt to be wanting.

Mr. Wharton scribbled some notes, and addressed himself once more to John.

'Do you mean to say that you never asked the prisoner if she had paid the money?'

'I took it for granted that she had.'

'And did you, a man of business, not ask for the receipt?'

'All receipted bills, by whomsoever paid, were strung upon a file in my father's study. Had I thought about the receipt of the £50, it would have been to conclude that it was there with the others.'

'Are you prepared to state that the notes, making up this £50, passed through no hands but your own and the prisoner's?'

'I have stated all I know,' answered John, evidently getting tired, but too well-bred to show it.

'Please to be explicit, witness. Do you positively state that the notes passed only through your hands and Miss Freake's?'

'I do positively state it,' said John icily.

'You can go, sir,' said the counsel. 'I have nothing more to ask.' Whereupon John stepped out of the witness-box; and, exchanging grave salutes with his acquaintances, passed from the respectful and admiring eyes of the crowd.

Next in order Mr. Smithson was called. His evidence did not amount to much, but it was chiefly confirmatory of John's.

Had asked to be paid in notes as more convenient; had thought it strange when the money was not forthcoming, but had refrained from pressing out of his great respect for the Hatherley family. Then occurred the lamented death of the head of the house, which made him still more unwilling to mention so trifling a matter as a forgotten bill. But yesterday, chancing to meet young Mr. Hatherley in the street, he had ventured upon a reminder, when Mr. Hatherley said he had sent him the money several weeks ago: Mr. Russell, who was arm-in-arm with Mr. Hatherley, had confirmed this. Upon being asked how Mr. Russell had confirmed this, the witness said that Mr. Russell had exclaimed in surprise:

'Why, I saw you give the money to Miss Freake for Smithson two months ago. You remember, I was standing by the carriage at the moment?' And Mr. Hatherley said that he remembered it perfectly.

'Did not the prisoner call at your house that day, within an hour of her receiving the money for you?' questioned Mr. Wharton.

'Yes. But I was out.'

John Hatherley was recalled, and asked if he had no knowledge of the £50 having been diverted to some other use than the one originally intended. He denied it.

'Did not Miss Freake mention to you that same evening that she had not paid the bill, Smithson being out: and did you not on the following morning authorize your coachman to ask the prisoner for the money?'

'By no means.'

'Then if the £50 were applied to some purpose other than the payment of Mr. Smithson's account, you did not know it ?'

' Certainly not.'

Most of the hearers felt quite disposed to echo John's quiet denial. It seemed so ridiculous to suppose even for a moment that he would order his cousin to do one thing with the money, and his coachman another. Ridgeley, the coachman in question, was not at hand, and Mary's evidence was next taken.

She had been sitting in the room reserved for witnesses, agitated and sick at heart; her sympathizers attributed it to her distress for her cousin, and to the natural shrinking of a young girl from publicity. In truth, she was dominated but by one thought : the terror of betraying herself. The necessity of concealment now had closed upon her like an iron band. She felt that there was no escape from it, and shrank with all the craven doubt of inexperience and stupidity from the thought of the cross-examination and its hundred pitfalls. Mary had at all times resented cleverness, and the cleverness of a lawyer was peculiarly to be dreaded now.

The aspect of the court with all the array of Justice congealed her blood with fear, so that her voice was hardly audible as she took the oath. But the respectful manner of the cross-examining counsel soon restored her self-possession. It seemed a kind of assurance to her that she would not be found out. With calm, returned cunning—the instinct of self-preservation—she denied knowledge of every-thing ; nobody had been more astonished than herself when the prisoner was arrested. The lie, once made concrete to her by the telling, was easy to maintain, and the cross-examina-tion of Mr. Wharton availed not to shake her in it. The testimony of John gained ad-ditional force when confirmed by the lips of this beautiful and haughty-looking girl.

Evening had drawn on, and the court rose. It was settled that the case should be re-sumed the next morning at ten o'clock, and Marleyford went home to dinner in a condition of pleased expectation. Nobody had heard the low, anguished moan of the prisoner when she was removed.

Already the torturing hours had left alive in Martha but one sentiment: a longing, distilled to agony, to know the worst and have rest. Anything—she felt, rather than thought —even the solitude of the prison, would be better than this procession of witnesses against her. The familiar, unfamiliarly cruel faces of her accusers had come to have a kind of spectral and altogether unendurable horror for her, and she panted for any catastrophe which should end it all. A kind of stupor fell upon her, but it brought her no relief, for a dull sense of betrayal beat in a surging, ceaseless tide upon her confused brain.

Meanwhile, Mary returned home in the carriage with her brother. Having dressed for dinner and eaten it, and warmed herself comfortably by the splendid fire in her luxurious but sombre drawing-room, she began to feel a little perfunctory remorse.

' John, what about the insanity?' she asked
when he joined her. ' When will they begin
to plead that?'

' Perhaps not at all.'

His tone made her angry, for she dimly felt
that the only object of his answer was to
annoy her.

' You know,' she exclaimed, ' it was only
on that understanding that I consented—I
mean that I——'

' That you determined to sacrifice Martha
and save yourself ?'

Mary sat speechless.

' There is still time for you to confess the
truth,' continued John coolly.

' If you think it so easy to tell, why do you
not tell it yourself ?' flashed out his sister.

He shrugged his shoulders.

' I suppose I have still a superstitious reverence for the Hatherley name.'

She beat an impatient tattoo with her foot,
feeling once again almost capable of rushing
off to Mr. Ormerod and confessing everything,

just to spite John. What was that abstraction—the family name—to her? Nothing. She thought only of herself. But — what would be the result to herself of her own tardy confession? For the fiftieth time her coward soul sank within her, at the vision of disgrace.

However, if she could not be courageous, she could be feebly vindictive and indignant.

'I should like to know the real truth about Ridgeley and that £50,' she said.

'You will know soon enough. Ridgeley will be the first witness called to-morrow.'

Mary sat looking at her brother—an angry light in her eyes.

'You are a fiend!' she burst out at last.

'You are mistaken. I am simply a man who pursues his own ends.'

John rose as he spoke, and Mary, with a peevish sigh, renounced open revolt, and gave up all thought of penetrating the mystery of Ridgeley.

The trial was resumed on the following day,

Ridgeley being first called. He stated that he had been several years in Mr. Hatherley's service as groom, had left, and returned on being promoted to the post of coachman. He knew nothing about the bank-notes spoken of; had never seen them, never handled them or known of their existence, far less had he used them. No denial could be more explicit or complete; nevertheless Mr. Wharton rose with a curious air of suppressed, expectant triumph.

'Did you not come into Miss Freake's sitting-room on the morning in question, and tell her that Mr. John Hatherley had ordered you to ask for the money, to pay a certain stable account?'

'I did not,' answered Ridgeley.

'You did not! Did not the prisoner tell you that she had the exact sum, but that it was destined to pay Smithson; and did not you reply that Mr. John wished the stable account to be paid first?'

'I can remember no such conversation,' replied Ridgeley stonily.

' What! Do you persist in declaring that the prisoner was not induced by these representations to hand over the £50 to you?'

' I never received £50 from her, sir.'

' But you frequently did receive as large, and larger, a sum of money from Mr. John Hatherley?'

For the first time a faint hesitation rippled the surface of the witness's dogged calm.

' I used to pay bills for Mr. John,' he answered.

' What sort of bills ?'

' Bills connected with the stables and the horses.'

' Did not Mr. John Hatherley about that time give you £20 ?—and £10 a month or two previously? Did he not give you small sums varying from £3 to £5 on several occasions?'

Ridgeley, now obviously somewhat shaken, was inclined towards doubt and forgetfulness at first; but was brought at last to admit that such had been the case.

'For what purpose were these sums given you?'

Apparently Ridgeley had not asked his young master. Mr. John Hatherley was very open-handed.

'Indeed!' ejaculated Mr. Wharton drily. 'Did not his open-handedness in regard to yourself begin six years ago last August, when you accompanied him to a church in the Strand?'

At this there was a decided stir in the audience. They detected a mystery, and for the first time that monument, the Hatherley 'legend,' slightly trembled on its base.

'Were you not a witness to Mr. John Hatherley's secret marriage?' continued Mr. Wharton.

Ridgeley answered 'Yes.' But his answer was a small matter; lost, as it was, in the tremendous commotion caused by the question.

John Hatherley married? Secretly? Six years ago? In the Strand? Never had there been such a buzz of comment, such a sea of astonished faces. The ushers had some trouble in restoring silence.

Mr. Wharton resumed his interrogations. For the third time John was summoned, and with what inquisitiveness may be easily imagined! But he was quite equal to the occasion. His self-possession was unshaken, only a shimmer of suppressed but profound emotion faintly irradiating the surface of it.

Questioned as to his relations with Ridgeley, he stated that he had known him for years: as a little lad: he had respected the man: that he had frequently made him presents, but that he had never authorized him to obtain from Miss Freake the £50 set aside for Smithson, nor had he any reason to suppose that he had done so. It was quite true that Ridgeley (who was not then in his service) had been one of the two witnesses to his private marriage. Neither would he attempt to deny that he had rewarded the man handsomely for his services, and his silence.

'Are we to conclude that your reasons for keeping your marriage a secret were weighty?'

'They were rendered weighty simply by the peculiar opinions of my father,' answered John. 'He had an extraordinary shrinking from all persons afflicted by——'

The young man for an instant paused. Only an instant, yet time for a hundred crowding recollections of old Mr. Hatherley's peculiarities to leap into the minds of many people who were present.

'Afflicted by physical infirmity,' resumed John, with pain. 'And my dear wife is unfortunately deaf and dumb.'

His voice rang with a mournful cadence. The revelation was so unexpected and so dramatic, that there was not one of its hearers but felt filled with pity. The pathetic, yet true and purely domestic fact had intrinsically but slight bearing upon the trial; but it brought the general sympathy strongly towards John. Further questioning elicited from him that his wife was now very ill: that this cir-

cumstance alone had delayed his introduction
of her to his friends since his father's death ;
but that he had made arrangements for bringing her down to Marleyford the very next
week, and that he had not hitherto announced
her existence—he really hardly knew *why* he
had not done it. It might be from the habit
of concealment—it certainly was no longer from
the desire of it. This explanation, vague as it
was, gave the impression that John Hatherley
knew his own affairs, and was capable of con-
ducting them.

The witnesses called in Martha's favour
were principally persons who spoke to her respectability and her general good conduct,
with others who had known various members
of her family and testified to epilepsy in one,
eccentricity in another, and to her own remarkable delicacy and abnormal shyness as a
young girl. A medical man said he considered
her very ' strange ' now.

Mr. Wharton's appeal for his client was so
earnest as to be almost impassioned. He

dwelt on Martha's blameless life, on the in-
timacy in which she had lived with the
Hatherleys, and the extreme improbability of
her being afraid to confess the loss, even if it
had happened, of the sum of £50. Was it
not more likely that she in her trusting simplicity had been induced, as she now declared,
to hand it over to Ridgeley, though the man,
for his own purposes, chose to deny the fact ?
In regard to the other and principal charge
against her, what was more intrinsically likely
than the story which she told ? Was it not in
accordance with all that was known of her
that she should have been made the tool of
another—though she shrank from disclosing
who that was? Mr. Wharton here made skilful
use of the supposed taint of insanity in Martha
to explain her dumb, dog-like fidelity, her
silence before the magistrates, her concentrated
terror of demeanour, and imperfect defence.

But the deftly-woven web of justification
fell to shreds beneath the Judge's summing
up. For if Martha were indeed a tool, then

who had employed her? John? He was the prosecutor. Mary? The idea was absurd in itself, even if Mary's own denial had not disproved it. Had not Mr. Hatherley and his sister and the coachman, one and all, told a perfectly coherent and credible tale? It was for the jury to consider which of the two stories was the most probable: a favourable one which would represent the prisoner in the light, first of the cat's-paw, and then the victim of an anonymous, invisible friend; or another which would show her as seeking to repair a probable act of carelessness by an offence whose serious consequences had presumably failed to strike her.

The jury took some time to consider their verdict, and on reassembling found the prisoner guilty; but in consideration of her hitherto unblemished character, recommended her to the mercy of the court. And the Judge, in passing sentence, said that he wished to make it as light as possible, and condemned her to six months' imprisonment.

Asked if she had anything to say, Martha looked up. A nervous trembling that had possessed her for hours suddenly ceased. Her frail little figure straightened itself, and over her pathetic face fell a light as from some vision seen of her alone. She raised her hand with a gesture so solemn that those who watched her were awe-struck and listened breathlessly for her words. Her lips parted : she was about to speak, when suddenly a convulsive shudder shook her frame. She threw her head back despairingly, cast her wasted arms towards the cruel immensity of the heavens, and with a cry of exceeding sorrow fell forward in a death-like swoon.

'Do you know what she reminded me of ?' said a young girl who had turned pale with pity. 'One of those pictures of saints, who in the moment of martyrdom see some sign in the skies : and then, when her face altered in that awful way, it was as if the sign had vanished, and nothing was left to her but the reality of her torture.'

CHAPTER VI.

CHANGES.

ARLEYFORD was moved to pity on hearing that when she recovered from the long syncope following her condemnation, Martha Freake was undeniably mad. 'A condition of strong cerebral excitement,' the doctors called it, and she was removed from prison to an asylum.

The next subject of interest that arose was John Hatherley's wife. She arrived with little Mark, her beautiful son of five years old; was introduced by her husband to her future home, and gratified expectation to an unforeseen degree. For she was exquisitely graceful,

gentle, refined; and, alas, condemned to die!
Consumption told its tale plainly in her wasted
form and sunken cheeks. Gliding about the
house in these cold spring days, wrapped
always in a white fleecy shawl, noiseless, mute,
uttering her thoughts but by signs, Mrs.
Hatherley was more like a phantom than a
living woman.

She had strangely-lovely, shining eyes, with
so intense a spirituality in their depths as to
awe, while it attracted, almost everybody who
came near her. John himself was *truer* in her
presence: and the one person whom she
seemed rather to fret than to elevate, was Mary.
The superiority of this pure nature, veiled by
infirmity and illness, irritated the girl's sullen
love of ease: in addition to this, she, herself
so faultlessly and coldly handsome, had inherited something of her father's dislike to
physical defects. Yet Mrs. Hatherley's afflic-
tion had nothing in it that should have raised
aversion even in the hardest nature, for it was
entirely the result of an accident which had

happened to her as a child. But what helped
to increase Mary's dissatisfied feelings towards
her sister-in-law, was the haunting sense of a
likeness in her to some face of which she could
not distinctly recall the identity. This impression came upon her so strongly at times,
that she seemed just on the brink of recollection. And strangely associated with this
vague memory was the idea, equally indefinite,
that the resemblance, if it existed, would have
some special importance.

One evening, Mrs. Hatherley being better
for the first burst of really warm weather,
John had invited some friends to dinner. In
the course of the evening he took them all
into the library, to show some of his latest
book acquisitions.

One of the guests, Mr. Ashbury — a
stranger in Marleyford, and more interested
in pictures than in books—began looking
about him, and paused at last before the portrait of an old lady, with grey hair covered
by a black coif.

'A fine portrait,' he commented. 'One of your family, Mr. Hatherley?'

'My grandmother.'

'A fine portrait,' repeated the connoisseur, 'and a fine face. Your grandmother must have been a beauty.'

'Her daughter, your aunt, was the handsomest girl I ever saw,' suddenly remarked Mr. Wilmot, one of the oldest inhabitants of Marleyford, turning towards John.

A rather awkward silence followed. Everybody knew that about the lady referred to there had been a story: and a clause in Mr. Hatherley's will had lately brought all the circumstances vividly back to people's minds. His sister, Rachel Hatherley, had been the first black sheep of the family. She had eloped with a distant cousin, who bore the same name as herself, but had been a humble dependent in his boyhood on her father's bounty. The young couple had been got off to America, and then Rachel's name had become a dead letter. Her father and brother never forgave

her, nor would consent to know anything
about her or her numerous children. But
John, when quite a young man, had gone to
Philadelphia after a defaulting clerk, and there
had come across his cousins. The details of
his acquaintance with them had never trans-
pired, but apparently he had been more inti-
mate with them than his father liked. For the
will, now just proved, under which he inherited,
was dated almost immediately after his return
to England; and it distinctly provided against
his marrying his eldest cousin, Margaret Hatherley. Disobedience on that point was to
result in total disinheritance. This condition
had recently given the gossips something to
talk about, and had surprised even Mary. For
she had been a schoolgirl at the time of
John's absence, and the very fact of his
acquaintance with his disgraced relatives
had been kept secret from her. She had
learnt it for the first time when the will was
read.

'You have no portrait of your aunt?' re-

sumed old Mr. Wilmot, with the obtuse per-
sistence of age.

'A miniature merely,' replied Mary. She
opened an old bureau and produced the miniature, not without some secret triumphant
consciousness of its being like herself.

Mr. Ashbury took it, and gave a little start
of surprise.

'Where have I seen the original?' he exclaimed. 'Let me think! Yes. . . . No.
. . . I have it. It was in America, twenty-
five years or more ago. A beautiful young
woman, the wife, I think——' he paused and
glanced hesitatingly, not liking to complete
his sentence.

'The wife of a bookseller,' blundered old
Mr. Wilmot eagerly. 'To be sure; that was
she.'

'This is very like you, Miss Hatherley,'
continued Mr. Ashbury, his eyes still fixed upon
the miniature. 'It is remarkable how the
family type has clung to you all.' His eyes
reverted to the portrait of the grandmother :

then to Mrs. John Hatherley seated in a high-backed chair beneath it. She was unheeding, because unhearing, of what was said around her. Her lovely eyes were fixed in reverie, her hands lay folded tightly on her lap. Over her head, to protect herself from the draught of an open window, she had drawn a black lace scarf. 'There is a strong family likeness between you and your brother and *all* these portraits. I declare,' he added, laughing, 'even Mrs. Hatherley has at this moment a likeness to your grandmother.'

Mary gave a great start—a start so unmistakable that Mr. Ashbury almost dropped the miniature in surprise. John, who had apparently not been listening, crossed the room at this moment and spelt out on his fingers a warning to his wife that she was sitting too long by the open window. 'We will go back to the drawing-room,' he said, addressing his guests, and drew his wife's hand within his arm.

'Tell me,' cried Mary suddenly, with extraordinary eagerness, to Mr. Ashbury, 'Did you know much of my aunt in America? Had she many children? Did you see them?'

John had drawn aside to let the party defile in front of him. 'Mr. Ashbury,' he said, addressing that gentleman with a courteous wave of his hand towards the door.

'She had only one child when I knew her, I *think*,' Mr. Ashbury was saying in answer to Mary. 'Let me see . . . . What did I hear afterwards about the child? a charming little girl, I remember. It died, it seems to me, in some odd, terrible way. Or was it only——' He paused, musing.

'Some strange accident?' suggested Mary, white to the lips.

But evidently Mr. Ashbury's memory for faces was very superior to his recollection of facts. 'I don't remember,' he replied, shaking his head; and aware of John's smiling summons, he at last obeyed it.

Mary tried to resume the subject later in the evening, but he evidently did not like to be cross-questioned. He only became more vague the more she interrogated him ; and the wild possibility which had presented itself and turned her faint with the rush of attendant thoughts, receded every moment into a dimmer and more distant background.

Nevertheless, she could not sleep all night, but tossed restlessly from side to side. And in the morning, when John had left the house, she presented herself in her sister's dressing-room. Mrs. Hatherley received her with her usual gentle sweetness of look and manner.

With characteristic apathy and selfishness, Mary had given herself very little trouble to master any means of communication with the dumb woman. She could speak a very little, slowly and laboriously, on her fingers ; and eagerness made the task easier for her now than in general. Only she questioned in a clumsy, blunt way, not as she would have questioned a person who could speak.

'Are you sure that your father's name was Lyndon?'

9—2

'Of course,' Mrs. Hatherley signified in reply, with evident astonishment.

'And you always lived in London?'

'Always, after he came home.'

'Home? From what place?' Mary's heart began beating again.

'From America.'

'Were you there with him?'

'Yes.'

'And how old were you when you came away?'

'A little older than Mark here,' and Mrs. Hatherley laid her hand tenderly on her little son's curly head.

Mary gave a sigh of disappointment, as she fixed her eyes, full of a fierce curiosity, on the pure, lovely face before her. Was she prevaricating to her, this wife of John's? The idea was too preposterously insulting even for her to accept it. She had nothing more to ask, yet would have begun to question again. But Mrs. Hatherley was very unwell that morning, and she lay back on her pillowed chair so motionless from weakness as to seem asleep. Mary had no choice but to leave her.

She spoke about it to Ralph Mercer ; but he condemned it as fantastic ; a foolish, visionary idea.

' You never heard that one of your aunt's children was deaf and dumb?' he said : and Mary was fain to confess that she had not.

' One might set a detective to work, if one had money,' mused Ralph. ' Not that it's likely to be true. Without money, hang it ! one cannot do anything—and you never have a spare sixpence, Mary.'

' That is not my fault,' answered Mary, with rather resentful significance.

John made her a very large allowance for pocket-money, but Ralph Mercer borrowed the greater part of it. His engagement to Mary was no longer opposed by John, and, except when mysterious errands took Ralph to London, he was for ever at Hatherley House. People began to talk a little, to

shake their heads too, to wonder what the
beautiful Mary *could* see in him to love.
Truth to say, it was a question which Mary
once or twice of late had asked herself. Her
obstinacy appeased by the withdrawal of opposition, Ralph lost a great part of his charm
in her eyes. Moreover, his doubtful life in
London during the year of separation, had left
an ineffaceable trace. In air, manner, and
speech he was distinctly more dissipated than
of old. His good looks, once very marked,
were obscured, and with his free-and-easy
ways, and his eternal debts, he was about as
unattractive a wooer as could well be imagined.

And in constant contrast with him was
Walter Russell: so refined, and gentle, and
clever: unswerving also in his affection, and
now the presumptive heir to his uncle's
baronetcy.

Given these two sets of opposing forces,
with nothing but Mary's fast-fading inclina-
tions to strike the balance in favour of Ralph,
and one can easily imagine the result. The

day arrived when his need of money became insupportable; when not ruin alone threatened him, but ruin accompanied by disgrace; and Mary engaged herself to Walter Russell. This took place within six months after Mr. Hatherley's death; but Lady Russell, writing from Carlsbad, while offering her warm, delighted congratulations, urged that the marriage should take place immediately.

'Sir Charles was already so much better,' she wrote, 'that the doctors really began to entertain hopes of his ultimate recovery. And it would give both him and herself so much pleasure to welcome the young couple on their return from the honeymoon, at Russell Hall. If your dear uncle continues to improve so rapidly,' wound up her ladyship, 'I shall feel as if I were returning with him from a honeymoon myself, for he looks ten years younger, and the change in him is altogether miraculous.

'What delightful news!' exclaimed Walter Russell.

'Delightful,' echoed Mary slowly. 'I suppose, Walter, that your aunt will herself present me in the spring.'

Walter was sure that she would do that, or anything else that could bring pleasure to his love. It was curious how devotedly he loved Mary—he as clever as she was stupid ; as true as she was false ; as brave as she was cowardly ! Her stately beauty and composed manner, the grace that resulted in her firm and perfect physical harmony, to his enchanted eyes were warrant sufficient for crediting her with a shining human soul. He was one of those men who do not care for any superfluous endowment of brains in a wife, but are content that she should be ' womanly,' having no very definite idea of what they mean by that elastic term. The wedding-day was fixed ; and in the preparation of her trousseau, the reception of her presents, and the congratulations of her friends, Mary was nearly happy.

' Do you know,' said John one morning to his sister, looking up from the perusal of a letter, ' Martha is well again—is cured ?'

'Cured?' Mary stared blankly. What would be the consequences to herself?

'So far cured,' continued John, 'that the doctors at the asylum consider that they can no longer keep her shut up. But they recommend absolute quiet and freedom from anxiety.'

'And the prison authorities—her sentence?' demanded Mary.

'The time of her sentence has just expired.'

'And what do you mean to do? Is she to be allowed to come out?'

Mary asked the question in quite an indignant tone. For after all Martha had been mad; she would probably become so again.

'I am afraid I cannot persuade the asylum to keep her,' replied John, with one of his quiet, covert sneers. 'Don't alarm yourself, Mary. Nobody would believe her story now. You are quite safe.'

'I suppose you have yourself to think of, as well as me,' exclaimed his sister angrily.

That was one of the things that most exasperated her about John—his cool assumption
always that the only peril of exposure was
hers.   After all, he was as criminal as she ; he
had known it was she who was guilty, and not
Martha.   If only John would be kinder to her!
But nobody ever was kind, except Walter—
for whom, in her secret soul, she had some
slight contempt.   There was, however, consolation in the thought that she should reign as
a queen when she became Lady Russell.

The marriage-day dawned at last, a splendid
morning.   The parish church of Marleyford,
between guests and spectators, was full to suffocation.   Rarely had so grand a wedding
been seen there.   Between the number of the
bridesmaids, the splendour of the dresses, the
full choral service, and the three officiating
clergymen, it was enough to make the dead
generations of Hatherleys rise from their
graves, in protest at such oblivion of their
stately sobriety.

But Mary had willed it so, being one of

those women who would hardly think themselves married at all without the orange-
flowers, Brussels lace, and wedding-cake, about
which they have dreamed for years. She had
gone about her preparations with an almost
religious solemnity, and carefully studied all
the most fashionable novelties. One of the
results had been to make little Mark her train-
bearer, and dress him up in a costume of the
time of Louis XV.

The service was over, and the bride and
bridegroom had paced down the aisle to the
spirit-stirring strains of the ' Wedding March.'
Mary stepped into the carriage, and proceeded
to release her train from the hands of little
Mark with all the reverential regard due to so
many yards of magnificent texture. Walter
stood smiling down at the child, and looking
happy and handsome in the sunlight.

The bridesmaids, one shimmering, fluffy,
airy, radiant confusion of lace and swansdown
and bouquets and pretty faces, were grouped in
the porch ; behind them were crowded ladies

in satin and velvets, old gentlemen with bald heads and rubicund faces, young men in glossy coats and lavender ties, with favours in their button-holes.

Suddenly, through the cloud of gaping rustics, a shabby, trembling, tiny figure made its way.

'Good-bye, Mary,' it cried; 'I wish you joy.'

And the bride fell back in her carriage with a shriek of absolute terror, as she recognised the face of Martha Freake.

The unexpected apparition caused no small consternation. Several young ladies fairly echoed Mary's scream; and John, hastily dropping from his arm the hand of the frightened Mrs. Ormerod, hurried towards the intruder with an air of dignified determination.

'Pray do not look so alarmed; I mean no harm to anyone,' said Martha. 'I only came down from London to fetch my things. I did not know it was Mary's wedding-day.'

She stood, turning her head from side to

side as she spoke, with a kind of childish curiosity.

'How can this be permitted!' exclaimed John, for once so taken aback that he hardly knew what to say.

'Oh, let me go!' wailed the bride from her carriage. 'Walter, send her away. She is mad. I am frightened. Why will people be so unkind?' Her voice broke into a sob, and she burst out crying.

'She is not mad, sir; only a little flighty-like and queer,' said a respectable woman who now addressed John. 'She has been staying with Mrs. Parsons, in London, since she was released; but she would come down to-day to fetch her own things from your house. Sometimes she seems half to forget what has happened.'

Still turning her head about in bird-like fashion, and without appearing to notice what was said, Martha scanned the groups around her. All at once her face changed. A shadow darkened it; her head fell. She put her hand up to her temple with a gesture of suffering.

'Let me go,' she said. 'There is too much noise here.'

'Lawks, ma'am! nobody is speaking,' said her companion pityingly.

'Too much noise. Too much noise,' repeated Martha, and turned away.

'She often says strange things, with no sense in them, sir,' resumed the woman to John. 'But she is quite quiet, and more manageable than a babe.'

The crowd shrank away, and Martha passed quickly out of sight. In the afternoon, when the wedding-breakfast was quite over, the same woman came to Hatherley Hall to fetch her things. Miss Freake would not come herself, she told John, although at first she had been so keen to do it. On their getting back to the inn, she had lain down at once and gone to sleep. She often did that after anything had seemed to trouble her, and was always restored by it.

John, however, wrote to the lunatic asylum protesting against his cousin's release, saying that he had seen her, and that she seemed anything but cured. In answer, he was told that Miss Freake on quitting the asylum was as sane as himself.

John thereupon journeyed up to London and saw Mr. and Mrs. Parsons, to whom Martha had returned. But Martha had already departed for Paris, and had insisted upon going alone. She was a little odd in manner at times, they added, and occasionally did eccentric things. But she had no delusions, and was never violent.

John Hatherley obtained Martha's address in Paris, and wrote to her, offering her a substantial monthly allowance. He received in reply a curt refusal, so little like the letter of a lunatic that he felt disposed, after reading it, to attribute Martha's appearance and behaviour on Mary's wedding-day rather to a spirit of revenge than to insanity.

CHAPTER VII.

WINIFRED.

TWENTY-FIVE years. It is a large span out of a lifetime; an age, seemingly, to look forward to or to look back upon. That period of time has nearly elapsed since the scenes recorded in our story, and the former chapters were but the prologue to what has now to come. Its thread is taken up in Paris; to which gay city we must carry the reader for a very brief sojourn.

Everybody who saw her for the first time was struck, not alone with Winifred Power's beauty, but also with her air of happiness. Not that she looked beaming, or facetious, or vacantly amused : nor was she perpetually laughing and talking. But she had an air of bright, resolute energy, which one instinctively felt could arise from no other source than a perfectly contented spirit. Her cordiality of manner, her fearless blue eyes, her quick blithe ways said plainly that in all her life she had given more of sympathy and help than she had needed.

Judgments, of course, differed about her as about everybody, but the majority of them were favourable. Among the weak, the poor, and the oppressed, indeed, Winifred counted a legion of friends. Not that people ever really disliked Winifred. Only some found her a little absolute, and others rather failed to understand her; and very sensitive, shallow, and vain persons thought occasionally that she had meant to affront them. Winifred was always dreadfully sorry when she discovered (which she did not always) that she had hurt anybody's feelings. But it is not certain that her sorrow was altogether conciliatory, for it had a slight mixture in its kindness of astonished, good-humoured, but faintly imperious scorn.

As a rule, it must be confessed Winifred had 'not very much time to trouble herself about people's feelings—as such. If they demanded consolation, sympathy, or active help (especially the latter), her energy indeed seemed as elastic as her leisure. But as long as those around her were satisfied, what she liked best of all was to have plenty of time for her painting.

For Miss Power was an artist, and no unsuccessful one for her years ; and the sums produced by her painting counted for something in the not always abundant family finances. Winifred lived in Paris with her uncle, Mr. Russell, and his wife. Upon the second marriage of his widowed sister in India, Mrs. Power, to Captain Chandos-Fane, the Russells had adopted the little girl, Winifred.

Latterly Mrs. Chandos-Fane, now a widow for the second time, had joined them in Paris.

The Russells had gone gradually down in the world. We last saw them at Marleyford in all the grandeur of their wedding-day. Ill-luck seemed to have tracked their footsteps. An heir, born unexpectedly, had deprived Walter Russell of his expected baronetcy. The failure of a bank had taken from him much of his own fortune. Ill-health had been his portion. And only a year or two ago, the treachery of a friend for whom he had been responsible involved him in difficulties. Then the fine apartment in the Rue Rivoli was given up for one in the Rue des Beaux Arts, a very different quarter. As compared with many of those around it, it was fairly handsome and commodious : and relics of their prosperity filled it : ormolu clocks, buhl cabinets, and—Mrs. Russell's lamentations. She liked magnificence—costly dress, and a handsome carriage to make her calls in : and, in a degree, she had this still. Intensely selfish was she, as in the times gone by.

On this day, when we first make Winifred's acquaintance, the late March afternoon, drawing to its close, found her, as usual, busy at her easel. Sitting by the bright wood-fire in a lounging-chair was a lady, whom few would have guessed to be the young artist's mother. Mother and daughter, indeed, were both fair; but there the resemblance ceased. The girl was tall and bright and active-looking; the elder woman was petite and languishing.

The difference between them was the difference between a pure white statue and a Dresden china shepherdess. Winifred, severely simple in attire, fair, flaxen-haired and beautiful, owed nothing to art. Mrs. Chandos-Fane, elegantly dressed, and elaborately coiffée, was a manufactured article of remarkable prettiness. She was nursing a white Angora kitten and reading Baudelaire's poems. For she was æsthetic, and declared that her daughter's pictures were not always 'interesting.'

'That is the third time you have sighed, my love. You are overworking, I am sure,' she presently remarked, in a cool, refined voice, laying down her book with a delicate yawn.

'I am not easily overworked, mother; and the picture *must* be finished by next week.'

'*Must!*' echoed Mrs. Fane. 'There you have the fatal destiny of pot-boilers, my child. I have always told you, and I repeat, that you will never be a good artist until you have ceased to work for money.'

'We must first cease to need money,' answered Winifred rather brusquely.

'Ah, well!' exclaimed Mrs. Fane: and it was wonderful how the indefinite ejaculation conveyed by its tone that no problems were insoluble to persons of superior nature.

Winifred set her lips a little tightly, and an expression less of grave annoyance than of deliberate self-control for a moment clouded her bright young face.

'I am not sighing because I am fatigued,'

resumed she, after a pause ; ' but because my
uncle is of late so manifestly worse.'

' We must call up strength of mind to re-
sign ourselves to the inevitable,' replied Mrs.
Fane, stroking the kitten's tail. ' We cannot
expect him to grow better, Winifred.'

The door at this moment opened to admit
a stout, cross-looking, yet elegant woman,
who entered, dragging her fur mantle after
her. It was Mrs. Russell. Handsome she
undoubtedly was still : but few would have
recognised her for the once beautiful Mary
Hatherley.

' I am so tired !' she said fretfully, sub-
siding into the nearest chair. ' The weather
is quite mild to-day. What a fire ! The room
is suffocating,' and she looked towards the
closed windows.

' I find it cold indoors,' remarked Mrs. Fane
placidly ; and she did not offer to let in any air.

' Is there no tea ?' asked the new arrival,
peevishly.

' I think there is a cup left,' answered Winifred's mother, glancing carelessly at the little Japanese tea-service on a low table at her elbow.

'I am too tired to pour it out for myself,' said Mrs. Russell.

Mrs. Fane put the kitten's paws round her neck and began talking to it softly. Winifred laid down her palette and brush and poured out the tea in silence.

'I have a piece of news for you,' said her aunt to her as she took the cup. 'Richard Dallas is dismissed from his employment.'

'*No!*' Winifred stood in consternation.

'I always thought that would be the end of it,' observed Mrs. Fane, who had never thought on the subject in any way.

'I drove there this afternoon,' resumed Mrs. Russell, 'and found them in great distress. I believe that the cause of his dismissal is some disgraceful discovery.'

'Disgraceful to Dick? I don't believe it,' exclaimed Winifred.

'Don't you, my love?' remarked her mother.

Winifred asked a string of eager questions, but Mrs. Russell was hopelessly vague. Naturally indolent now, her intelligence at this moment was additionally obscured by fatigue. She leaned back in a condition of irritable somnolency, from which Mrs. Fane roused her at intervals by stirring up the fire.

Meanwhile, Winifred, as soon as her painting was brought to an end by the failing light, scraped her palette and thrust her brushes into water with unusual haste. The Dallases—an improvident, unfortunate family —were her great friends; and her affectionate imagination conjuring up vividly all that they must be at present enduring, she prepared to rush off to them with characteristic impetuosity.

All at once came a violent ring at the outer door, followed by the equally violent entrance of a young and very pretty girl, but by no means a good-tempered-looking one. The puckered brow and angry eyes of this saucy, piquante brunette betrayed a disposition the reverse of mild, and, at this moment, apparently heated to explosion-point.

'Oh, Gerty! I have heard the news,' said Winifred sorrowfully.

'Good-evening, Miss Dallas,' said Mrs. Chandos-Fane, icily reproving.

'What a noise!' exclaimed Mrs. Russell.

Undisturbed by these manifestations of various feeling, Miss Gertrude Dallas cast herself into an armchair, mutely irate, and began beating the floor with her pretty foot.

'I am so distressed,' whispered Winifred.

Gertrude shrugged her shoulders cynically.

'It is just our luck,' she answered.

'Can nothing be done?'

'A great deal. But we, my dear Winifred, are not the people to do it.'

Having delivered this remark, in a tone of bitter sarcasm, Miss Dallas folded her hands, fixed her eyes on a corner of the ceiling, and resumed her tattoo.

'Would you kindly explain what has happened?' asked Mrs. Fane.

That was soon done. Richard Dallas, Gertrude's half-brother, older than herself, and born of a French mother, had, through the interest of his maternal relatives, obtained a post as sub-curator to a provincial museum in France. The appointment, as conferred on a half-foreigner, had always excited some jealousy, and Richard had never hit it off with his immediate superior. Lately, some valuable Syracusan coins were discovered to be missing. The loss was probably of old date, the museum being very carelessly managed. But it had only been now found out: a scapegoat was needed, and personal spite found a vent in the choice of Richard Dallas.

'That is just the whole story,' said Gertrude, bringing her curt narrative to a conclusion.

'How disgraceful!' breathed Winifred.

'Very *unfortunate*,' observed Mrs. Fane politely, with a slight stress on the adjective, that brought an embarrassed blush to her daughter's cheeks and an angry stare to Gertrude's eyes.

'Dick is only the victim,' affirmed the latter, as if in answer to an unspoken accusation. 'It is the head-curator who is to blame. The Municipality should be written to; the Government memorialized; the——'

'Who says all this should be done?' interposed Winifred quietly.

'*I* say so,' flashed out the other angrily.

'Was it a sweet, white, soft, beautiful, *beautiful* kittensy, and did it never have to memorialize anybody, except its mistress, for a wee-wee saucer of milk?' lightly chaunted Mrs. Fane, tilting the Angora up on its hindlegs, and looking at it with a fascinating smile.

Gertrude sprang up; the indifference irritated her beyond control. 'I am going, Winifred.'

'No, you are not,' returned Winifred with gentle authority, taking her two hands and forcing her back into her chair again. 'You are to stay with me and be in some sort comforted, you poor child. Only you are to try and talk a little practical sense, for our behoof as well as for your own.'

'What practical sense can I talk?' flamed out Gertrude. 'Of what use can I be? Am I not a cipher, a nonentity; in other words, a young lady? Lady, forsooth! Much good there is in being that, when one must toil and grind from morning to night like—like a crossing-sweeper. And everybody the while to cry "Peace" where there is no peace, and to preach patience when patience is only a cloak for incapacity.'

'How very magnificent! Where did you learn all that?' laughingly retorted Winifred, her sense of fun getting momentarily the upper hand of her compassion. But Gertrude was tragic: in the presence of that eloquent kitten she had no resource but to be earnest. To be anything less was to be ridiculous: and ridicule was the one thing that Gertrude Dallas most feared on earth.

'It is very well for *you* to talk,' she answered sulkily. 'Who ever interferes with you?'

'A difficult question to answer,' remarked Mrs. Russell.

'Yes, indeed. Our dear Winny rules us all,' spoke the mother.

Winifred looked down, but said nothing. She was as little given to self-pity as to self-praise; nevertheless at this moment a vague revolt against injustice stirred faintly within her. The thousand small sacrifices of herself to which she owed her ascendency—who was there to appreciate them?

'There it is,' pursued Gertrude triumphantly. 'Winifred can do as she pleases. You can make use of your talents; work unhampered——'

'But surely you could work also, if you liked?' interposed Mrs. Fane, with an innocent air of seeking for information.

'Yes, as a governess,' replied Miss Dallas scornfully, turning a dusky red in her exasperation.

This governess question was a very sore
point, as she had tried the career and igno-
miniously failed. Of course, through no fault
of her own: when were the Gertrude Dallases
of this world anything but the victims of
adverse circumstances ?

'I could spend my youth shut up in a stuffy
schoolroom with detestable children of wooden
intelligence—I could do that, of course,' pursued the young lady, with magnificent contempt. 'Or I could sweep a crossing, or go
about with a basket selling pins and staylaces,
or—in fact there is no end to the occupations
which I might find if I *chose.*' The accent on
the last word was withering.

'Some governesses get a hundred a year,'
put in Mrs. Russell.

'Very probably. In some eyes, doubtless,
a human machine is priceless,' retorted Gertrude, with defiance.

'Are not *you* priceless?' exclaimed Mrs.
Fane to the kitten, which put out one velvet
paw and tapped her on the cheek.

'Good-evening,' said Gertrude abruptly; and she rose, pale with annoyance, and left the room. Winifred went with her to the stairs and took leave of her sorrowfully, promising to come as soon as dinner was over.

'We shall be glad to see you, of course,' replied her friend, not very graciously. 'But I am afraid you will not find us very lively company,' she added, and ran lightly down the stairs.

'What you can see to like in that ill-tempered girl passes my comprehension, Winifred,' remarked Mrs. Fane.

'All Winifred's friends are eccentric,' said Mrs. Russell plaintively.

'Wait until you have seen Mademoiselle Marthe!' laughed Winifred. 'Then indeed you may talk of eccentricity.'

'You are always threatening us with that person,' exclaimed Mrs. Fane. 'Who *is* she?—and when is she definitely to appear?'

'When I have succeeded in vanquishing her

shyness,' replied Winifred, 'and I can't do that yet.'

'I am sure you had much better leave her alone,' observed Mrs. Russell. It is too Quixotic to consider yourself bound by ties of eternal gratitude to a queer, probably vulgar old woman, just because she happened to show you a little attention when you were ill.'

'She nursed me with the greatest devotion, and she is not vulgar,' retorted the girl.

After dinner Winifred prepared to start, her maid Sophie in attendance, for the Rue Ste. Catherine, where the Dallases dwelt. But before leaving, she tapped at a door at the end of the corridor. 'Come in,' said a voice, and Winifred entered her uncle's bedroom. A pleasant room, although it was the home of an invalid, and although its denizen knew no change but the slow advance of a mortal malady, and no variety but such as consists in spending one's bad days in bed and one's better ones on a sofa.

'Ah, my Brunhilda! Whither away?' said

Walter Russell, looking up from the review he was reading by the light of a shaded lamp. The name—given her playfully in allusion to her fair, tall beauty—and the tone in which it was pronounced spoke volumes for the cordial friendship, deeper than mere relationship, which reigned between the sick man and the girl.

'I am sorry I shall not be here to read to you this evening,' said Winifred, seating herself beside her uncle's couch; 'but I must go to the poor Dallases. You have heard of their fresh misfortune?'

'Yes, poor things! Fate has a spite against them, as it always has against the feckless: if, indeed, one should not rather say that the feckless have a spite against fate,' added Mr. Russell, with the half-wistful smile of a man whom evil fortune has made a philosopher.

'Now, what is the meaning of that? Something cynical, I am sure.' And Winifred shook her golden head reprovingly.

' Only as Nature is cynical, my child.   The feckless are clearly intended by natural laws to sink ; yet the Winifreds of this world, with a great expenditure of energy and pity, persist in helping to keep them afloat.'

' You know those are the things I don't like you to say, Uncle Walter.   And I believe that one day the Dallases will find out how to help themselves.'

' You believe that?   Then you have a great deal of faith.'

' Are you better to-night ?'

She took his wasted hand tenderly as she asked the question, and bent down to look into his face with anxious, loving eyes.

' I am better,' he said, ' for I am nearer the goal.   Nay, do not look so sad, child.   You are very good to grieve for me ; but glance beyond your loving regrets, and ask yourself what I have to live for.'

' For your friends,' murmured Winifred.

Yet even as she said the words, even as she

drew the noble, grey head to her and laid her
soft young cheek upon the massive forehead,
regret for a moment died down in her,
quenched by self-forgetful pity. Her uncle had
been all in all to her. The books that she
had read with him gained an added significance from his comments ; and his intellectual
companionship had educated her as no books
alone could have done. Yet, above the
passionate longing of her love and her youth
and her strength to keep him with her always,
rose the sympathetic comprehension of his
sorrows. Of how little books and the love of
friends, the voice of pity and the touch of
tender hands, can be to a man who, stricken
now with physical helplessness, and embittered
with the sense of failure, looks back along the
traversed track of life, and sees his baffled
efforts standing phantom-like with regretful
eyes of pain! Keeping back resolutely an
unwonted rush of tears, Winifred pressed her
lips upon the sick man's brow, and in that
kiss, for that moment, resigned him almost

gladly—*almost!*—to the peace and silence of the tomb.

'Go—and come back quickly,' he said. 'And perhaps there may still be time for you to read me a page or two of our book. Your touch must be magnetic, Winifred. Something that you meant that kiss to say to me seems to have done me good.'

She did not find much to say in answer to that, but left him, promising to make haste. On her way downstairs she met Claire, the young flower-maker, who lived two stories above her, and who was helping her blind grandfather to climb the steep flights.

'Bon soir, mam'zelle,' simultaneously said the girl's fresh tones and the old man's quavering treble, as they became aware of Winifred's presence. They were neighbours, these two girls, and had come to like one another much, although their intercourse was principally limited to nods from their respective windows, and the one was a young gentlewoman, and the other but a poor flower-maker. Claire, sitting

at her work in her humble room, could look
down into Winifred's studio. Sometimes the
young artist, brush in hand, would appear at
the window, just for the sake of throwing
a bright smile of greeting upwards. And
often, in the early morning, for both rose with
the lark, Winifred would be hanging out her
canaries just as Claire appeared at her own
casement with her blackbird. And Winifred
declared that this same blackbird had been the
source of much inspiration to her. For its
first liquid notes echoing through the court
seemed to be the herald of the spring. Then
many an aching head and a flushed, weary face
was lifted from its occupation of needlework,
or watchmaking, or copying. Windows were
thrown open, just through the infection of
gladness, and those condemned to stifling
rooms and imperfect light through the dreary
winter days, knew that soon the first tender
shoots of green would brighten the town
gardens, and the Marché aux Fleurs be fragrant
with violets—not forced in hothouses, but

gathered in the woods! It was these homely touches, reminders of the poetry of poverty and the holiness of work, which made her life in Paris dear to Winifred.

CHAPTER VIII.

MR. DALLAS, the unfortunate Richard's father, was one of those charming people who make everybody uncomfortable, and are universally adored. He was a perplexing unknown quantity in the lives even of his nearest and dearest: a fantastic element, with which they could never cope, and constantly disappointing expectation.

There was never any telling what Mr. Dallas might do next—except fail. For fail he invariably did, in whatever he undertook. It was a brilliant kind of failure often, for he

had plenty of talent. But the results, when
they came to be inspected, were none the less
dismal for having had a sort of phosphorescent
splendour. He was a painter, a musician,
a poet, and had produced creditable, albeit
unfinished work in all lines. Only, through
some queer perversity of nature, he never produced it when wanted. If a picture were
ordered of him, he set about composing a
poem. If an editor (by some unheard-of
stroke of good luck) were found to consent to
read a poem, Mr. Dallas would discover that
he had nothing good enough to show him:
he would promise something better, and meanwhile set to work on a song. Such industry
as he had, and, to do him justice, he was
rarely idle, seemed to recoil from the task
appointed to it.

For the rest, Mr. Dallas had all the facile
grace of his temperament, and fascinated every-
one. If nobody on a closer acquaintance
entirely believed in him, on the other hand
nobody ever entirely disbelieved in him. The

most sober-minded and the most hardworking
of his acquaintance had an infinite patience
with him; and, perpetually helped by their
efforts above the immediate consequences of
his own imprudence, he looked down with the
smiling serenity of an all-unconscious self-
complacency upon the toilers who supplied his
wants.

'I am so glad to see you, dear,' said kind-
hearted, short-sighted Mrs. Dallas, receiving
Winifred with open arms. 'You have heard
of our sad trouble. Take off your hat and
have some tea.'

The good little woman's fetish (for all
divinity had long vanished from the idol) bore
the sweet name of 'home.' Only, 'home'
with her meant really dining at one o'clock
and having raspberry jam at tea. That was a
delicacy which had soothed her children's angry
tempers when they were little: she could not
conceive that it should fail in a similar effect
now that they were big. Their aberrations
perplexed her, as all aberrations did equally,

from house-breaking to undarned socks ; but when she beheld them gathered round the hissing urn, the evidence of their discontented countenances never availed to convince her that peace did not reign in their hearts.

'I have just dined, but I will take a cup,' replied Winifred, knowing that to refuse was to break her hostess's heart. 'Where is Dick?'

'Gone out for a little stroll, poor boy ; but he will be home to tea,' said Mrs. Dallas cheerfully. 'Mr. Dallas is in his studio, hard at work. He has had an order to paint Monsieur and Madame Dubreuil's portraits; they are to be finished in a month, for their daughter's birthday.'

'And is he painting them by lamplight?' asked Winifred, in great astonishment, yet pleased at the news.

'He is preparing some etching-plates, and starts on an etching tour to-morrow,' explained Gertrude, with a kind of sulky irony.

'Poor papa! He is always so busy,' remarked simple Mrs. Dallas.

' He might be busy to better purpose, just now, mamma.'

' Your papa knows his own affairs best, you may be sure, my dear.' The little air of matronly dignity with which this reproof was administered, and its own intrinsic, affectionate imbecility, secretly exasperated Gertrude. But for once she subsided into silence, after no stronger protest than an expressive toss.

' Well, what are you all about? Is tea not ready? Ah! Good-evening, Miss Winifred!' said Mr. Dallas, rubbing his hands with the bearing of a man who has achieved a task and is pleased with it.

' We are waiting for poor Dick,' said Mrs. Dallas.

' Wait for no one. Punctuality is the essence of success. There is no defect for which I have so profound a contempt as un-punctuality,' observed he, turning towards Winifred.

This in the presence of a domestic calamity would have astonished Winifred, could any-

thing in Mr. Dallas have astonished her. As
it was, she only said gravely, ' I came to con-
dole with you about Richard.'

' Ah, Richard! poor lad!' Regret clouded
the father's open, handsome countenance. ' He
has been infamously treated, Miss Power. Infamously. I have written out a petition.
Perhaps a better plan would be to horsewhip
the curator? I think I will go to Blois to do
it. By Jove! I will start to-morrow,' wound
up Mr. Dallas, struck with the sudden idea.

' And your etching?' suggested Gertrude.

' The etching be hanged! it can wait,' replied
her father, with serenity. ' Here's Richard.
We were going to begin tea without you, my
boy; you are five minutes late.'

Richard, a dark, slender, and attractive young
man, came forward and shook hands with
Winifred in silence. He was looking sad and
pale.

'I am so sorry for you,' she murmured.

' I am sorry for myself, but there is little
help in that,' he said, glancing at her grate-

fully. 'I suppose I am fated to go to the wall.'

Gertrude, curled up in an armchair, here gave a derisive laugh. 'We are always going to the wall, all of us. In fact, we live in an *impasse*,' she observed amiably.

'In the absence of more effectual effort, my child, you can continue to console yourself by making epigrammatic remarks,' said Mr. Dallas, not well pleased.

Gertrude looked furious; she hated reproof. But in any war of words with her father, she knew that she was always beaten, though she had inherited much of his caustic wit.

'Where is the cosy?' inquired of the world at large Mrs. Dallas, peering about painfully.

'It was left in the drawing-room. Georgie, go and fetch it,' commanded Gertrude of her younger sister, a lanky maiden of fifteen.

'Go yourself!' retorted Georgie, who was nursing a splendid cat, the mother of Mrs. Chandos-Fane's kitten.

Enraged to activity, Gertrude sprang up

and made a dart at the rebel. Georgie ducked; the cat bounded; Mrs. Dallas's key-basket was upset, and its contents were scattered upon the floor. She stooped to collect them, caught a corner of the table-cover, and some of the cups fell with a crash to the ground.

'Gertrude!' cried Mr. Dallas, turning his anger upon her. 'Go to your room, and stay there.'

'*I!*' Gertrude exclaimed. 'I?'

'*You,*' replied her father. 'When you are by, there is neither peace nor quiet of late ; neither decent behaviour nor civil speech.'

The girl stood for one moment transfixed with amazement and a bewildering sense of wrong. Then, as an ill-timed and triumphant giggle from the appeased Georgie met her ear, she turned and rushed away, banging the door behind her.

Winifred made a movement to follow her, but Mr. Dallas interposed. 'Let her be, for Heaven's sake,' he said. 'But that insanity is unknown in our family, I should really tremble sometimes for that child's future reason. Her storms of passion are unbearable.'

Poor Mrs. Dallas, with trembling hands, and murmuring that *this* time it was not Gertrude who was in fault, restored something like order to the tea-table, rang the hand-bell for fresh cups, and invited everybody to sit down. She crept away presently with Gertrude's tea to the culprit's room, but returned in a grieved way, shaking her head. The door was locked, and she had been denied admittance.

Except by herself and Winifred, Gertrude was not missed. Mr. Dallas himself was in delightful spirits. He always was thus in the presence of family misfortune ; that was one of his peculiarities. He even rallied Richard, who sat abstracted and silent, and launched out into brilliant disquisitions on things in general, and all that he intended to do with them.

Tea over, Winifred rose to go. ' I will call

Gerty. She would be so sorry not to say good-bye to you,' said Mrs. Dallas eagerly.

Winifred knew that the goings and comings of the entire world were at this moment matters of supreme indifference to the indignant Gertrude. But too good-natured to contradict, she waited.

Mrs. Dallas returned, looking disturbed. 'Gertrude's room is empty,' she cried. ' She must have gone out.'

' Alone? and at this hour!' exclaimed Mr. Dallas.

' Well, I cannot find her.'

Gertrude had slipped out unobserved. Hortense, the servant, and Winifred's own maid, in high converse in the kitchen, had heard the outer door close softly, but did not know who had gone out : had thought it was one of the gentlemen.

' I expect she has only gone to the Bonnards',' suggested the mother, the Bonnards being great friends of Gertrude's.

' But she ought not to go at this hour,'

said Mr. Dallas. Presently the bell tinkled, and 'Here she is!' they exclaimed. However, it was not Gertrude, but a note from her to her mother, brought by a commissionaire, who said there was no answer.

Mrs. Dallas opened the note ; then stood up scared and speechless. Richard took it from her.

'Read it out,' said Mr. Dallas to his son : and he obeyed.

' " I relieve of my presence a home where, by your own confession, my part is that of a firebrand. Domestic life being, so far as I am concerned, a failure, I intend in future to live away from you. Before this reaches you I shall have left Paris. Do not try to find me. It will be useless.—GERTRUDE." '

Horror-stricken, they looked at one another. Then Richard rushed away to overtake, if possible, the commissionaire, and Mrs. Dallas and Georgie began to cry. Winifred sat dumb ; Mr. Dallas walked up and down the room. He was less frightened than angry :

such a proceeding as this of his daughter's grated, he would have told you, on his fine sense of order.

When Richard returned, breathless, he had failed to find the messenger. Mrs. Dallas felt quite sure that the only people to apply to were the Bonnards, that Gertrude had gone to them ; and Richard again departed. He came back, again unsuccessful, but bringing with him the astonished and dismayed Monsieur Bonnard. He, bald-headed and decorated, a respectable and kind-hearted Frenchman, was quite overcome at Richard's news, and had arrived to offer his services.

' They had not seen Mademoiselle Gertrude for some days,' he said. ' He was quite sure she had not been even for a moment at their house that evening. Their only visitor had been Lieutenant Valéry, who had called to take leave.'

' Lieutenant Valéry !' exclaimed Hortense, who, French servant-like, had come in to listen. 'Was he an infantry officer, monsieur?

A little young man with a reddish moustache, and black bright eyes ?'

'Mais oui ; mais oui !' that described him exactly.

'Then Mam'zelle Gertrude has run away with him,' Hortense boldly declared.

Mr. Dallas uttered an exclamation of incredulous anger ; Monsieur Bonnard one of horror ; Mrs. Dallas breathed a sigh of relief. *Her* simple mind immediately conjured up a romantic love-story, tears, forgiveness, blessings, a trousseau and general happiness. The men, more alive to practical difficulties, took a different view.

'Run away with him !' indignantly repeated Mr. Dallas. 'How dare you say so, woman ! Who is the fellow, Bonnard ? I never heard of him before.'

'He visits at our house. I am afraid your daughter has met him on occasions there,' groaned Monsieur Bonnard.

'All I know is, they meet in the street sometimes ; the other day, when I was out with Mam'zelle Gertrude, they had a long conversation,' affirmed Hortense.

' We must go after them,' exclaimed Mr. Dallas, starting up. ' Dick, you come with me. Where is this Valéry to be heard of, Bonnard ?'

' He starts to-night for Lyons, on leave, mon ami '—and the kind-hearted old Frenchman, looking deeply concerned, took the agitated father aside. ' A French officer of that rank cannot marry unless he deposits 25,000 francs at the Ministry of War. Valéry has not a sou.'

Mr. Dallas looked at him with scared eyes, hardly understanding. The vivid colour, which excitement had brought to his face, slowly receded.

' The chief point is to pursue them as quickly as possible,' urged Monsieur Bonnard, pressing his hand.

Ten minutes later Mr. Dallas and Richard had left the house, taking with them all the money they could scrape together. They were accompanied to the station by Monsieur Bonnard.

But on arriving there they found they had just missed the Lyons night express by five minutes ; and they had, in consequence, no choice but to wait with such patience as they could until morning. Part of the night was spent in making inquiries ; and they were able to establish with tolerable certainty that a young couple answering to the description of the fugitives had indeed started by the express.

Winifred meanwhile had lingered a few minutes with the idea of comforting Mrs. Dallas. But to her surprise the little woman needed but slight consolation.

' Poor dear Gerty, she has been rather head-strong at times of late. Perhaps you may have noticed it ?'

Winifred, who had never noticed anything else in all the years of her acquaintance with her friend, murmured a vague assent.

' It often puzzled me,' pursued Mrs.

Dallas placidly, 'puzzled and pained me. But now it is quite explained. The poor child had this love-affair in her head. If she only had placed confidence in me, I might have made it all smooth with her dear papa.'

This new view of Mrs. Dallas, as a person of influence in her own family, severely tried Winifred's gravity. But the unconscious pathos of it touched her also.

She went home with a heavy heart. Even while hoping for the best, she had ten times Mrs. Dallas's knowledge and experience, and was proportionately removed from the possibility of taking the same sanguine view. And quick of sympathy always, she was more than ever disposed to grieve where Gertrude was concerned. The two girls had been friends from childhood, and Winifred loved the wayward nature that was so far beneath her own. She made excuses for Gertrude's violent temper, and exalted the fitful generosity which at times redeemed it. For, of all the many illusions of life, what spell is more potent while it lasts, more irrecoverable when it has vanished, than the tender glamour of early friendship ? Half-way down the hill of life we look backwards along sunny meads, and onwards into gloom. Above us, there on the flowery slope, appears a radiant form : is it our youth ? Is it our early friend ? Before we know, the gracious phantom had vanished ; and, beckoning down the rugged path, stands the austere, veiled maiden called Duty.

Two or three days of suspense ensued, during which the story of the flight oozed out, and raised a great hubbub round poor Gertrude's name. Then Mr. Dallas wrote briefly to say that he had found his daughter, and would soon be returning.

' With her, of course,' said Mrs. Dallas ' Dear papa ! I wonder if we shall like the poor young man.'

She pitied Lieutenant Valéry without exactly knowing why. Probably she pictured him to herself as tremendously in love.

When Mr. Dallas and his son appeared, however, they had a very unexpected story to tell.

Gertrude had run away with the young man, not out of love, but from sheer reckless- ness. Smarting under her father's reproaches and under the fancied wrongs of years, so exaggerated in her imagination just then, she had quitted her home with the intention of taking refuge in the first instance with the Bonnards. Further than this she did not know what she should do, and perhaps in her excitement did not care. The Bonnards might want to force her back to her home. Such a prospect filled her with fury and despair.

In front of the Bonnards' house she had ran up against Valéry, who was leaving it. She had met him several times, and her haughty vanity had been gratified by his evident ad- miration. In a world which did not appre-

ciate her, even the homage of a French lieutenant of foot was a drop of comfort.

He stopped in much amazement at seeing
her alone at such an hour, not putting the best
construction on it.

Her confused, passionate answers to his
questions only increased his doubts; but he
listened to her with that curious mixture of
incredulity and pity which a man of his
stamp accords to a woman's narrative of her
wrongs.

To make a long story short, he presently
proposed to her, perhaps three parts in jest,
to accompany him to Lyons. Impelled by
some demon of crazy recklessness, she accepted
the invitation.

She took a savage pleasure in compromis-
ing herself in the eyes of her family, and of
consequences she had at the moment but a
very confused impression. In her inexperience and her arrogance she believed she could
keep herself perfectly straight and defy the
world.

The alarm, the angry disappointment of
her awakening, constituted the bitterest,
because the first *real*, lesson of her life. A
very few hours of Lieutenant Valéry's society
sufficed to fill her with detestation for
him; and she no sooner found herself in Lyons
than she ran away for the second time, leaving her companion extremely astonished and
aggrieved—feelings later considerably aggra-
vated by the horse-whipping inflicted on him
by Mr. Dallas, and for which that gentleman
refused him satisfaction.

As for Gertrude herself, the state of repen-
tant excitement in which her father found her
was pitiable. She would not hear of marrying
Valéry: even before the horse-whipping, and
supposing that he had desired it. She would
not hear of returning home. She supposed
her character was damaged, she informed
them, folks were so ill-natured; but her people
themselves were to blame. She reproached
her father, her brother, everybody; and poor
Dick had ever been a good brother to her.

She wept, she stormed, she was tragic and
pathetic, simply by force of her mental perversity. The strength of her conviction, that
she was a victim, was a rock on which all
argument broke.

'I must make shipwreck of my life now in
any case. Yes, I *choose* to do it. Let me
take my own way,' she reiterated: and Mr.
Dallas, worn out by anxiety and anger, fairly
succumbed at last to her violence. Her plan
was to go to Turin as teacher in a school. She
knew of such an opening, as it chanced, and
might as well begin her series of failures there
as anywhere else. So Richard was sent to
escort her to Turin, and Mr. Dallas returned
to Paris alone.

The exact truth about Gertrude's flight, her
family naturally never told. Neither the
Bonnards nor Winifred learnt whether Hortense's suggestion of an elopement had turned
out to be correct. Nobody ever asked now
for Gertrude; and her name ceased to be mentioned.

Only Mrs. Dallas, when alone with Winifred, sometimes would drop her head upon the girl's shoulder and weep silent tears of disappointment and despair.

CHAPTER IX.

MADEMOISELLE MARTHE.

MRS. RUSSELL, as we know, complained that Winifred's friends were generally eccentric. And certainly the one about whose eccentricity there could be no doubt was Mademoiselle Marthe.

She was not French, but very English. Nevertheless, the very few friends she had, belonged to the country of her adoption, and none of them called her by her surname, or thought of asking what it might be. She was *the* Mademoiselle Marthe *par excellence* of the quartier. No one, before or since, had ever been seen like her. She had a tiny, wizened

body, a small, puckered face, and a still, half-
scared manner which contrasted strangely with
her wistful eyes. Something there was so
very human about her, that, looking well at
her, you felt inexplicably compassionate and
attracted. But any advance was chilled by
her unconquerable and painful reserve. ' She
is like a caged and frightened fawn; ' she looks
as if she had once been told a ghastly secret,
and never forgotten it,' were the various phrases
by which people strove to explain the odd impression which she made upon them.

And because she was incomprehensible, she
was, on the whole, more feared than thoroughly
pitied. Her pride, combined with her deadly
poverty, made the weak-minded a little resentful of her; and she sometimes excited the evil
fear of the malignant by sudden flashes of clear
perception and brief assertions of principle.
Her usual manner, half-frightened and very
depressed, gave place at moments to a pathetic
excitability. Something in her, long repressed,
seemed at times to rise in revolt against her

sad and anguished life, and sting her into a
feverish and short-lived activity. By profession she was a copyist of pictures : very humbly
and devotedly she trod in the track of great
departed artists, and seemed, for the most part,
quite devoid of any personal ambition. But
every now and again she appeared possessed
by an evanescent desire to achieve something
greater; and while this fit lasted she was wont
to make sketches of original paintings, and
exhibit them for approval to her fellow-workers
in the gallery.

It was the favourite amusement of some
mocking, ill-natured spirits extravagantly to
praise these attempts, and nothing could be
more touching than the expression with which
Mademoiselle Marthe would listen to their
words. Gratitude, unwilling doubt, the longing to believe, the desire to love, the sad, sad
secret sense of artistic incapacity struggled for
mastery in her half-childlike, ever-questioning,
and wholly mournful eyes. One day in the
gallery, Winifred being present, Mademoiselle

Marthe had been made, as usual, the butt of the rest. Marie Duchêne, the terror of everybody for her cruel tongue, Clara Smythe, an underbred English girl, and half a dozen others, had gathered in front of the sketch, and were exalting it in their usual style.

'C'est épatant!' declared Marie, in mock rapture.

'*Too* lovely!' added Clara.

'Look at the grouping!'   'The expression!' 'Ce coloris!'   'The feeling!'

Thus ran the chorus, accompanied by motions and gestures. Winifred, her back turned to them all, went on painting in silent indignation.

Presently, when the victim had gone away, Marie mockingly began upon her. 'Notre chère Winifred!   Does such genius render her jealous, or simply strike her dumb?' A general laugh greeted this.

Winifred turned. 'I think you should all be ashamed of yourselves,' she said quietly, but her blue eyes flashed like a sword in the sun.

There was a pause of amazement. 'Well, to be sure!' exclaimed Clara, with a toss of her head.

'Tiens! tiens!' murmured Marie, and made a grimace.

'I am quite in earnest,' continued Winifred, unmoved. 'I think you all behave disgracefully to that poor old woman. She is not very wise, but she is a gentle, unoffending little soul, who would not hurt a fly, and she does not perceive your ridicule, because ridicule finds no place in her own simple and kindly heart. She is full of reverence for the art which we all profess to follow, and although she never can succeed, because ungifted, her failure is a nobler thing than the facile degradation of talent which we pretend to honour as success.'

'Is that intended for me?' flashed out Marie Duchêne.

'For anybody whom the cap may fit,' answered Winifred coldly.

Then there was a sudden cry of 'Hush!' and the angry group turned to find Mademoiselle

Marthe standing behind Winifred, within hearing. She was very pale, and her aged baby-face had the pained look of her darker hours.

' I went out to buy galettes for you. Marie said she was hungry.'

She held out her offering mechanically, as mechanically as she had spoken the words. One or two of the girls had the grace to look ashamed. Marie, with an exaggerated air of gratitude, sprang forward to embrace the little artist; but Mademoiselle Marthe drew back.

' I do not want your kisses, my dear,' she said gently. ' Somehow, they have a flavour of your praise.'

She never showed anybody her sketches again ; and, indeed, by degrees she ceased to make them. The lesson had been too cruel, and the memory of its pain, abiding with her, gradually quenched the faint, flickering flame of her belief in her own powers.

She did not overwhelm her champion with any expressions of gratitude, but showed her affection by a hundred small signs. If they

were together in the gallery, she was never so
happy as when allowed to scrape Winifred's
palette, or wash her brushes, or run down to
buy her luncheon. The snow had hardly
melted from the ground before a bunch of
sweet-smelling violets was left in the early
morning, with the concierge, at Winifred's
house; and one Christmas Day appeared a
piping bullfinch, which Mademoiselle Marthe
had trained and taught through many patient
weeks.

In vain the girl sought to return these
kindnesses. Mademoiselle Marthe would accept
nothing from her, and contrived moreover to
give to her rejection a gentle dignity, in touching contrast with her usual humble ways.
Winifred herself was long before she ventured
to penetrate to the tiny room which the little
old maid called her home. When she did at
last see it, she was agreeably surprised by it,
for, although modest to the verge of bareness,
it had nothing sordid. The plain, scanty
furniture was scrupulously clean, and the

13—2

windows were bright with flowers and birds.

'And you have lived here all alone for more than twenty years!' exclaimed Winifred, wondering what the unspoken chronicle of the long, lonely life had been. 'You have friends— visitors?'

'I have friends—yes. Everybody is very kind to me. But I have no gentlemen or lady visitors, if that is what you mean. At least not until you came,' added Mademoiselle Marthe, with her faint but patient and pleased little smile.

Winifred, almost unconsciously, took her hand.

'But now you will make friends among your own people. You will come to see us?' she exclaimed, impetuously.

'My own people? I have none,' replied Mademoiselle Marthe. 'My kindred are the poor and suffering.'

The words had a sudden ring of pain, and a new expression swept over the speaker's

face. It was not anger, still less resentment;
it could hardly even be called bitterness. But
it was full of a fathomless and blasting woe.
Two burning spots had come into the wrinkled
cheeks, the lips quivered with an agitation
made all the more painful by the strained look
of the tearless eyes. She drew a little away
from her visitor, with a movement that un-
wittingly said how she shrank from commonplace compassion. Winifred began to talk
about herself, her aims, her friends, her
pictures, and thus drew to the surface that
unselfish sympathy which was the key-note
to the other's reticent nature. In time, Winifred thought, she would vanquish the little
woman's reserved timidity, and end by bringing about a meeting between her and Mr.
Russell. She ardently desired this : for,
dimly yet strongly feeling that Mademoiselle
Marthe had been in some way wronged, she
believed that her kind and clever uncle might
be able to learn the secret. But in this aim
she failed.

One day, indeed, Mademoiselle Marthe caught quickly at the name ' Russell,' which Winifred had for the first time mentioned.

' Is that your uncle's name? And *Walter*, did you say?' She turned rather pale, and seemed struggling to hide some emotion.

' Yes. Did you ever know him?' was the surprised question.

' Nay, there are many Russells in the world. And Walter Russells too.'

But even while thus answering, Mademoiselle Marthe looked strangely troubled. Winifred sat silent, expecting, hoping to be further questioned ; but no interrogation came, and Mademoiselle Marthe began to talk of something else. Nevertheless her manner remained wistful : and as Winifred, on leaving, stooped to kiss her, she spoke in a trembling way.

' Does injustice make you angry, child ? Could you be pitiful and loving even if the world reproached you for it ?'

' Of course,' replied Winifred.

To her surprise and consternation this answer provoked a burst of tears, the very first that she had seen in her friend. Tears are akin to speech: was the veil of this anguished past, whatever it might be, to be finally lifted?

No: Mademoiselle Marthe checked her emotion, almost as if ashamed of it, and drooped her head humbly.

'It is so long since I have cried,' she said, in her simple, patient way; and Winifred felt that the moment for questioning had not come.

With characteristic loyalty, she abstained from following up the clue, if such it could be called, which the agitation at the name of Russell might have seemed to offer. That is, she did not describe Mademoiselle Marthe's singularities to her uncle, or ask him if he had ever known anybody answering to such a description.

The friendship thus begun between the strangely-contrasted pair was destined, on Winifred's side, to be intensified later by gratitude. The previous summer to this when we first make her acquaintance, her uncle and aunt having gone to England, she joined several other artists at Fontainebleau. Mademoiselle Marthe was there also, although she could not be said to belong to the party. Presently small-pox broke out. Winifred fell ill. Fortunately her attack proved of the mildest; but it sufficed to scare away all her companions save one. The exception was Mademoiselle Marthe, who suddenly proved herself of rare efficiency. Feeling seemed to stand her in lieu of special intelligence; where suffering of any sort had to be alleviated, she always knew the right thing to do. And Winifred, tended by her with a limitless devotion, came to feel the moral superiority that was veiled by her persistent reserve. Formerly she had merely pitied Mademoiselle Marthe; now she respected and loved her. And when she got well, she thought she never could do enough to mark and proclaim her gratitude. The sight of such friendship stirred to malice the small souls of her fellow-students.

During one of Winifred's rare visits to the gallery, when they were all back in Paris again, Clara Smythe began another battle.

'It is a pity you were not here yesterday, Miss Power. You might have heard " something to your advantage," as the advertisements say.'

'To my advantage?' Winifred repeated, in surprise.

'Yes. That is, of course, if you consider it an advantage to be enlightened as to the true history of your friends.'

There was a general little giggle at this, the rest of the girls being prepared for what was to come.

'I must trouble you to explain yourself,' returned Winifred.

'Among the many kind of failures which you consider interesting, do you include the failure to keep out of prison?'

The colour rose in Winifred's cheeks.

'I am a bad hand at guessing riddles,' she said.

'Yesterday, my aunt, who was passing through Paris, came with me here,' resumed the spiteful girl. 'As we entered, your *protégée*, Mademoiselle Marthe, passed out. My aunt gave a great start of amazement on seeing her, for she recognised her as a person she had known once in England.'

'Yes?' repeated Winifred, wondering what was coming.

'And who was condemned to a term of imprisonment for writing threatening letters.'

There was a dead pause, then Winifred said coldly :

'I presume your aunt gave you some particulars as to names and dates and places?'

'Really, Miss Power, to be frank, I was too shocked to ask for particulars,' replied Clara.

'Then you must permit me to believe that your aunt made a mistake of identity. It could not have been Mademoiselle Marthe.'

And with these words, Winifred, who had already packed up her painting materials and made ready for her departure, turned her back and walked away.

' The Christian name was the same, at any rate ; and you can ask your friend if she has ever been in Kent,' called out Clara : but Winifred was already out of hearing.

For several weeks Winifred saw nothing of Mademoiselle Marthe, for Mr. Russell became very ill, and claimed all her attention. By the time he again partially recovered, great things had happened. The King of Prussia had turned on his heel and left M. Benedetti standing in the sunlight on the promenade at Ems : war had been declared, and the first shots fired ; and although France did not yet fully foresee the catastrophe in store for her, matters began to look serious.

The Bonnards were leaving Paris in some haste for their country house in Provence, and they invited Mr. and Mrs. Russell to accompany them. Winifred could not leave, for she had a picture to finish, and Mrs. Chandos-Fane had no fancy for French country-life. So she betook herself to Boulogne-sur-Mer, on the understanding that her daughter should join her there.

Winifred, thus left to her own devices, bethought herself one fine Sunday morning of Mademoiselle Marthe, and went off to see her.

' It is my birthday, dear,' said the girl, giving her little friend a hug. ' You cannot be so barbarous as to expect me to spend it all by myself. So you are just to come home and help me to eat the feast that Sophie has prepared for me. And afterwards we will go to the Bois and see the brides.'

Mademoiselle Marthe was nothing loth. She made herself ready with her wonted care; one of the most characteristic and touching things about her being the exquisite neatness of her poor attire. Winifred, watching her affectionately, thought she seemed brighter than usual, and was struck anew with the

childlike goodness underlying the age and
sorrow of her face.

They sallied forth, and the girl's gleesome
prattle, combined with the loveliness of the
day, kept up the pleased look in her companion's eyes. For many long and weary
years, indeed, Mademoiselle Marthe's dimmed
glance had not dwelt with such untroubled
peace on the serenity of the heavens. Such
moments are the ambuscades of fate : another
instant, and the blow falls.

All at once, the two friends came upon Clara
Smythe and a party of girl-artists. Winifred
would have passed on with a bow, but Mademoiselle Marthe, partly from innate courtesy,
partly from habit, stopped and held out her
hand. Miss Smythe, however, was equal to
the occasion. Drawing herself up with stony
dignity, she looked the little woman over from
head to foot. Then she dropped a courtesy.

'I think, madam, you must have mistaken
me for some old acquaintance from Marleyford,'
she said, and walked away.

Her victim stood rooted on the sunlit path, still as a graven image, an image of Pain. She uttered no word, no sigh even; but her face turned so ashen grey that Winifred involuntarily cried aloud in alarm.

'Come home, dear!' exclaimed the generous girl, quivering with indignation. 'Never mind what they say; just come home with me.'

The simple, ardent words fell upon unheeding ears. Mademoiselle Marthe mechanically allowed herself to be led away, but her awful silence remained unbroken. Only by a sign did she testify her wish to be taken to her own home instead of to Winifred's.

The latter, frightened at the unnatural calm, called a coach and put her into it. She went home with her; took off her dress; made her lie down; and petted her in womanly fashion. Then, not knowing what more to do, in a very passion of sympathy, she drew the trembling frame into her strong young arms, and kissed her friend in speechless pity. At the touch, Mademoiselle Marthe burst into a convulsion

of tearless sobs, which seemed as if they would
last for ever. Scared and powerless, Winifred
sent in haste for a doctor. He administered a
calming dose, and after a while the patient
dropped asleep. But she awoke at the end of
an hour or two, feverish and delirious. She
began to rave incoherently about her own trial
and the presence of Mary in the witness-box.

This one vision returned again and again
with singular vividness; it was plain that of
the many circumstances connected with her
betrayal, the treachery of her cousin had burnt
most deeply into Martha Freake's memory.
The piteous prayer for truth, only the truth,
reiterated every moment, seemed to tell its own
tale : and Winifred, listening through the long
watches of the night, registered a mental vow
that if redress could be had she would obtain
it. Her uncle and aunt came from Marleyford:
from them it would be easy to learn the whole
story.

Mademoiselle Marthe recovered. That is to
say, consciousness returned to her, and with it

something of her usual manner. But her face wore a constant look of torture, and instinctively Winifred felt that to question her would be like probing a quivering wound.

She consequently had no choice but to possess her soul in patience, and wait for some future chance of enlightenment. From her uncle and aunt she had failed to obtain information. Mr. Russell was too unwell to write, and his wife was one of those unsatisfactory correspondents who never answer questions. Finding that Mrs. Russell passed over the subject of Mademoiselle Marthe in silence, Winifred could but conclude that she had nothing of real interest regarding it to relate.

All this time events in the great world had been proceeding with startling rapidity. Sédan had been fought, the Empire had fallen, and the Prussians were marching upon Paris. There was a *sauve-qui-peut* among the foreigners, and Mrs. Chandos-Fane wrote to her daughter in hot haste to join her at Boulogne.

Winifred in her heart would rather have

remained where she was. To her, not fore-
seeing what was to happen, the prospect of the
siege held forth no terrors. Moreover, she
loved Paris, and felt all the inexplicable fascination which France, in her darkest as in her
brightest days, can cast upon the minds of
men. It was pain to her to quit, in such an
hour, the great city where she had dwelt so
long.

But Mrs. Fane's letter was imperative. That
lady possessed one of those indefinite natures
with which it is impossible to deal. On the
surface as airy as gossamer, as light as the froth
of the sea, she had a clinging tenacity of purpose which was not to be repressed.

Her present letter to Winifred was that of a
lonely and loving mother. 'I have but you
in the world, my child,' she wrote, in a delicate,
flowing hand. 'Since the death of your dear step-
father, since my dear little children, one after
another (your half-brothers and sisters, love),
were taken from me, my life has been desolate.
I say this in no reproachful spirit. You have

your art (as you call it) ; and you make some money by it; naturally you have slipped into the habit of being absorbed by it. But you must *sometimes* think of your poor mamma. I am sure I am not exacting. You generally have your own way, darling; and I think I am always indulgent. But France is no place at present for a young girl. No, not even for my wise Winifred . . . who *thinks* herself so wise! I am going to England, and I should like you to come with me. Some mothers might say they *required* it: but I only say I should *like* it. My Winifred, after a little re-flection, will perhaps see that the day may come when she will not be sorry she has some-times done something to please her loving

'MAMSIE.

'P.S. I have met Sir John Hatherley here, and with him the three ladies whom he has so *generously* received into his home. He is very nice. Much nicer than his sister, *I* think. But of course that is only my opinion. He

tells me of a charming cottage to let, close by
his own place. I should like to take it. But
mothers have to consult their daughters now-
adays.'

Winifred read this epistle with some perplexity and a dim sense of pain. Her sensitive
conscience made her very quick to blame herself and very much alive to reproach. She
quite seriously asked herself if she had ever
been wanting in love or respect to her mother?
Yet if she had not, what did Mrs. Fane's in-
sinuations mean?

There came a time of riper experience, when
she learnt that the gist of her mother's letters
had to be sought in their postscripts. But she
was too young and too generous to understand
this yet; and she felt vaguely dissatisfied with
herself the whole day.

The notion of disregarding her mother's
wishes, when so plainly expressed, never even
occurred to her. She packed her boxes with
all speed; took a sorrowful farewell of Made-

moiselle Marthe (whom no entreaties could persuade to leave Paris); a regretful one of the poor seamstress, Claire, and a mute one of all the familiar faces, all the well-known sights and sounds which had woven themselves into the many-coloured web of her student-life.

On reaching Boulogne-sur-Mer, she found Mrs. Chandos-Fane the centre of an admiring circle of devotees, who were disposed to regard Winifred herself with a lively interest slightly dashed with hostility. For while talking of her daughter, praising her daughter, longing (as she said) for her daughter's arrival, the widow had managed in some subtle, probably unconscious way, to convey that her daughter did not appreciate her. 'My beautiful Winifred'—'my clever Winifred'—'my terribly strong-minded Winifred,' were words never off her lips. And as a rule people do not like the 'clever or the strong-minded.'

She had a great deal to tell about Sir John Hatherley, and to this Winifred listened with

unfailing interest. Sir John, Mrs. Russell's
brother, was, people said, her benefactor. This
was never admitted by Mrs. Russell; she,
besides being of a generally aggrieved turn of
mind, considered herself particularly injured in
being left by her father's will dependent upon
her brother. Nothing that he could do seemed
sufficient compensation for this original injustice. But others, looking at things from a
different point of view, were disposed to think
that the millionaire did a good deal; for Mr.
and Mrs. Russell owed their principal means of
existence to his liberality.

Whenever additional money had been needed
by *her*, he was written to, and, as far as Winifred knew, he had never failed to respond to
the call. Personally Winifred felt grateful to
him, for much of her education must have in
directly been paid for out of his purse.

Winifred had never seen Sir John; but
she thought much of him, and always as a
good and great man. She had lived abroad;
in Italy, Germany, of late in France; he de-

tested the Continent, and it was a mere chance which had recently brought him to spend, for the first time in his life, a few weeks at Boulogne-sur-Mer. The bathing there had been recommended for his widowed sister-in-law, Mrs. William Hatherley; who, with her two daughters, dwelt under Sir John's roof, further recipients of his bounty, being themselves penniless.

'When I saw those three women,' said Mrs. Fane to her daughter, 'I must say that the admiration I had always felt for that benevolent man was increased a thousandfold. *Such* a woman, she! and the young ones, oh so frivolous!'

'Perhaps they suit him very well,' replied Winifred, not always disposed to accept her mother's judgments.

'No doubt you know best, love,' answered Mrs. Fane; 'but I believe you have not seen them? No. So I thought. Then, subject to your future correction, I may be allowed to give my opinion. *I* think they are quite un-

worthy to be the companions of such a man as
Sir John.'

' Is he so very cultivated, then?' asked
Winifred, a little subdued.

' *I* think so. I believe that a love of old
books is generally supposed to show a cultivated mind.'

' That depends upon whether the collector
reads them or not,' answered Winifred brightly.
' Sir John has always been something of a
Sphinx to me. From his letters to Aunt Mary
I never could make out what manner of man
he was intellectually.'

' You will soon know, my almost too-clever
daughter,' rejoined Mrs. Fane, with a smile
and a little pat on Winifred's cheek. I have
authorized Sir John to take for us the pretty
cottage I told you about. We shall find him
a delightful neighbour.'

In a very short while Mrs. Fane crossed the
Channel with her daughter and maid, to take
possession of this desirable cottage, which had
been made ready for them. It was in the

neighbourhood of Sir John Hatherley's residence of later years, and not too far from London. But on their arrival they heard that Sir John and his family were still away; and it struck Winifred that this piece of news curiously dashed her mother.

Mrs. Fane could console herself, if necessary, by contemplating Sir John's handsome residence, The Limes, its velvet lawns and its beautiful grounds. For the grand stuccoed mansion, placed on a slight rise, looked down upon the neighbourhood both metaphorically and materially. It was the largest and the finest house in the place, and the centre of much local social ambition: to be invited to it was an honour; to be shut out from it a reproach.

To Winifred, fresh from the roar of Paris, there was something very soothing in this suburban neighbourhood, with its pretty redbrick dwellings, with creepers climbing up them, and the flowers blooming in the beds behind the iron wickets. The neighbourhood was already a tolerably large one, and grew, alas! daily. But there was still a common; still a rustic-looking ale-house; still a genuine English lane or two, which echoed to the cry of the cuckoo in spring and the songs of nightingales in summer. And on each side of the lanes were buttercup-strewn meadows, where kine crouched beneath the shade, and rooks cawed in the branches of the noble elms.

Mrs. Chandos-Fane had time to unpack all her dresses, and Winifred to settle down to her work, before the shutters of The Limes were opened, and the butcher's boy and the baker's drove their carts with greater importance for the knowledge that 'Sir John' had returned.

CHAPTER X.

SIR JOHN.

THE church bells of the little village of Elmsleigh, sheltered in its quiet Surrey nook, were calling people to service on Sunday morning. Mrs. Chandos-Fane, while dressing herself with extraordinary care, cast glances of unusual scrutiny at her daughter's own attire. She suggested various youthful and airy additions, which the girl would not make.

'Never mind, mother,' said Winifred good-humouredly. 'It really does not matter how I look when you are by. You are elegant enough and pretty enough for both of us.'

' I hope I always look like a lady, my love,' said Mrs. Fane, contemplating herself virtuously in the glass. Nobody ever accused me of vanity, even when I was your age, although *I* did not affect to be indifferent to my appearance. But I confess I should like Sir John not to feel ashamed of his connections.'

' I dare say poor old Sir John will hardly look at us, mamma.'

Mrs. Chandos-Fane bridled.

' *Old!* He is not old, my love. But since any allusion to your benefactor displeases you —yes, I call him so—I will not make it. I have no doubt Mark will suit you better.'

With this, Mrs. Fane swam out of the room and the house, and Winifred silently followed.

On reaching the church and sitting down, she guessed by the frequent turns of her mother's head in what direction she was to look for the Hatherley party. But the service was on the very point of beginning before they appeared, and then Sir John was not with them. Only Mrs. Hatherley and her daughters, with Mark, Sir John's son. Winifred, woman-like, looked at the latter first. He was a grave, handsome young man, who evidently did not wear his heart upon his sleeve, but looked, nevertheless, as though he had heart and brains too. He recognised Mrs. Chandos-Fane, and raised his eyes quickly towards Winifred. For a moment their glances met, seriously, quietly, without a trace of consciousness. Then Mark turned his head away, and Winifred transferred her observation to the ladies. The mother, William Hatherley's widow, was an octoroon born in Jamaica, and looked like it. She was heavily dressed, even on this bright September morning, and had a trick of drawing her shoulders forward and shivering slightly, presumably under a visitation of draughts that afflicted nobody else. Between these trembling movements, her small, wizened face, and her bright, glancing eyes, she reminded one of a captive marmoset.

Her daughters were two rather pretty little

things, extremely alike, and very daintily
attired. Winifred wondered whether it was
only the proximity of Mark's massive brow
that made their delicate faces look so mind-
less. They glanced at her with ill-concealed
curiosity, and took evident stock of her costume from her bonnet to her boots.

At the church-door the whole party met,
Mrs. Chandos-Fane going forward with a
marked cordiality. The girls responded to it
with some shrinking, Mark with a calm polite-
ness, and Mrs. Hatherley—not at all.

'My daughter: she has been dying to make
your dear children's acquaintance,' said Mrs.
Fane to her. Winifred longed to contradict
her flatly, but feeling that to be impossible,
she gave her hand to them with grace.

'You have just arrived?' said one of them
to her, Dorothy, regarding her delicate gloves.

'Yes, just—haven't you?' echoed the other,
Florence, scrutinizing the severity of her
dress.

'I trust we shall have the pleasure of seeing

you often at The Limes,' said Mark, who had
been looking at Winifred with a composed
directness that half-amused and half-provoked
her. She conceived of him that he was a
young man who always did his duty, and
invited her and her mother now as a part
of it.

'We will call on Sir John this afternoon,'
said Mrs. Fane. Whereupon Mark shook
hands, raised his hat, and said, 'Good-bye,
then, until later;' his cousins nodded con-
descendingly, and Mrs. Hatherley murmured
something that was presumably a farewell.

'A more ill-mannered quartette I never
wish to see!' exclaimed Mrs. Fane, with an
acrid vigour of denunciation strikingly in
contrast with her usual suavity.

'Mark was polite and pleasant enough,'
answered Winifred.

Sir John Hatherley was the great man of
this small neighbourhood. People regarded
him with awe, and talked of his good fortune

with almost superstitious veneration. Originally he had been a brewer, but no ordinary one. For the brewery was an old-established, almost aristocratic affair: and he had been left by his father sole possessor of it, and a rich man besides. In a short time he sold the business and also his handsome house near Marleyford, and bought this place, 'The Limes,' at Elmsleigh. Then he engaged in railway speculations to a large degree; gained money upon money, applause, and the honour of knighthood. 'He is like a king,' said the admiring world; 'everything he touches turns to gold.' But he had his peculiarities.

Mrs. Fane and Winifred went to The Limes through the afternoon sunshine. Dolly met them in the hall.

'Hush, hush!' cried she.

'Hush!' added Flossie, coming forward.

'What is the matter?' inquired Winifred, very much astonished.

'You are passing the library,' whispered Dolly. 'Uncle John is resting. His heart, you know,' she explained, as she led the way to the drawing-room.

Winifred then remembered that Sir John suffered from disease of the heart, and was supposed to be living in a critical state.

On entering the room they found Mrs. Hatherley smothered in shawls in the depths of an armchair. She rose languidly, extended a tiny listless hand, and got as far as the first word of ' How do you do?' after which she sank back again.

' And your cousin Mark?' said Mrs. Fane, with sweet inquiry.

' He is out,' answered Dolly.

' Gone to town, I think,' said her sister.

A faint shadow of annoyance crossed Mrs. Fane's pretty face, but she said with undiminished feeling:

' And dear Sir John is unwell?'

' His heart, you know,' began the sisters together, when suddenly Mrs. Hatherley interrupted them.

'He ate too much pheasant-salmi yesterday,' she remarked in a drawling monotone.

At this unexpected observation, Winifred
absolutely started, and glanced at the speaker
with a new curiosity. But the pale little face
above the bundle of shawls was totally impas-
sive. Mrs. Fane looked unmistakably indignant at the remark, and said that invalids
were greatly to be pitied.

'Dear Uncle Hatherley suffers terribly.
And, as he always tells us, any agitation
might kill him,' said the elder of the sisters.

'The *least* agitation,' repeated Florence.

And both spoke in such evident good faith
that Winifred smiled on them with her bright
sympathy, saying kindly :

'I dare say he owes much of his ease to
your nursing.'

'Who would not willingly nurse such a
sufferer?' chimed in Mrs. Fane. 'I am sure
I would sit up night after night: although,
with my anxious temperament, I am aware
that I should pay dearly for it.'

At this amiable outburst it must be confessed that Winifred rather stared. Mrs. Fane had had plenty of opportunities of nursing her brother Walter, but she had certainly never availed herself of them.

'And are you very fond of nursing also?' suddenly said Mrs. Hatherley to Winifred, lifting her head from her wraps.

'Mr. Russell, as you probably know, has been a helpless invalid for years,' answered Winifred gravely.

'And I will say of my darling child that she is always most devoted to him. She has but one fault—if fault it can be called—that of being unwilling to let anyone, even *me*, share her task.'

Mrs. Chandos-Fane turned a glance of enchanting maternal sweetness on her exasperated daughter, but the expression suddenly changed on meeting Mrs. Hatherley's brilliant, monkey-like eyes. What did the woman mean by her impudent stare? she mentally asked—and Mrs. Fane repaid it with interest, her blue eyes meeting the black ones intrepidly : but she did not succeed in staring Mrs. Hatherley down.

At this moment the door opened to admit a tall, stately, and still very handsome man. With his black velvet dressing-gown, his black velvet cap, and flowing white beard, Sir John Hatherley—for he it was—might have sat for a picture of Prospero.

Winifred rose; Mrs. Fane hurried forward; Dolly rushed for a footstool; Flossie to shut the window. Mrs. Hatherley alone remained motionless and unmoved.

With a wave of his hand in acknowledgment to his nieces, a bend of his head in greeting to Mrs. Chandos-Fane, the master of The Limes walked straight up to our heroine.

'And who is this?' he asked in slow, melodious tones, looking down upon her with his magician-like air.

'My daughter, dear Sir John.'

'Mater pulchra, filia pulchrior.'

This compliment, accompanied by a stately

bow, would probably have afforded Mrs. Fane
but a moderate amount of gratification had
she understood it. As it was, she blushed
with enchanting sweetness; while Winifred,
standing there with her hand clasped in Sir
John's long and wax-like fingers, was regarding him with steady eyes of the frankest
astonishment. She was completely taken
aback by his appearance and manner; she
had expected a genial benevolence, a bluff
kind of genuine cordiality, but nothing like
this majesty, or this matchless . 'get-up in
velvet.' Sooth to say, she was but slightly
impressed. Possessing the touchstone of a
royal sincerity, she did not take long to
detect the dross of a nature that was not
sincere. And with the sudden rush of an
overpowering conviction, she was fain, albeit
reluctantly, to confess to herself that she
considered Sir John Hatherley was no better
than Mrs. Russell.

Quite unconscious of the impression he had
produced, the benefactor of so many people

responded to the general inquiries concerning his health with urbane resignation.

Probably he admired Winifred, for he addressed his conversation principally to her. He asked her, she noted, next to nothing about the Russells, but a great deal about herself. With a suave, fatherly manner he talked to her of her art, her success, and of art in general. She did not think he knew much about it, but listened respectfully. Everybody else listened also, and Winifred was quick to see that Sir John liked a hushed circle of auditors. Even when Mark came in, as he did presently, he took a seat in the background and remained silently attentive. It was quite like a lecture : and the resemblance was further increased by Mrs. Hatherley's going to sleep and Mrs. Fane's smothering a yawn or two, the girls meanwhile sitting both upright, with their eyes very wide open indeed.

Sir John was not long in getting off art to his bibliomania—that mysterious quality which

the neighbourhood adored in him without com-
prehending it.

Mrs. Fane eagerly professing interest in
Elzevirs and Aldines, he asked rather sharply
if she understood them: and on finding she
did not, graciously offered to exhibit his collection.   Upon this, the whole party adjourned
to the library, even Mrs. Hatherley gathering
together her shawls and shuffling tardily after
the rest.

One after the other the treasures were produced.   A 'Theocritus,' printed by Zacharias
Calliergi; a 'Romaunt de la Rose,' bound in
morocco, and stamped with the bees of De
Thou; an Elzevir 'Pâtissier Français' (worth
a fantastic price); an original quarto of 'Mac-
beth;' some plays in the rose-coloured bindings
of the graceless Du Barry; a 'Manon Lescant,'
illustrated by Boucher.

'For this,' said Sir John, unlocking a glass-
case and producing an illuminated Psalter
written in gold on a purple ground, 'for this I
paid £800.'

There was a universal exclamation. Even Mrs. Hatherley craned her neck towards the object with an air of unusual interest.

'It is very old,' continued its possessor, 'as you may see, or might if you understood, by the clearness of the writing and the grotesqueness of the figures.'

'I have heard that it is difficult to tell whether these Psalters are genuine or not,' said Winifred. 'What are the signs?'

A certain peevishness, if any term so flippant were admissible in regard to him, was visible in Sir John at this question. Contrary to the wont of most collectors, he did not seem to care to exhibit his erudition.

'The signs? They have to do with the catchwords. You would be a long while understanding them, my dear young lady,' he added, while locking up and restoring the case.

'Where is your illustrated 'Gerusalemme Liberata?' asked Mark. 'I want to show it to Miss Power. As an artist she will appreciate it more than any of us.'

'Why, Mark, I am sure I think it beautiful,' exclaimed Dolly, very naïvely aggrieved.

'Where is it, sir?' persisted grave Mark, with a slight glance at his young cousin.

'I have sent it to the binder.'

'To the binder?' echoed the young man in surprise. 'The binding was perfect, and of the early eighteenth century, I believe.'

'It was out of repair,' responded Sir John, still more briefly than before. Then lying back in his chair, he gently closed his eyes, raised his beard to a picturesque angle, and put his white hand feebly to his heart.

'Oh, he is ill!' cried Florence, and flew to his side.

'Eau-de-Cologne!' exclaimed Dolly, and vanished in search of it.

Mark, with an air of concern which yet had something perplexed about it, quietly opened a window, and then approached the invalid. He knew that these attacks might mean mischief.

Sir John waved his disengaged hand slightly.

'No fuss, I beg,' he murmured. 'The paroxysm is not severe; it will pass.'

Apparently in a few moments it did pass, for Sir John's fingers quitted his heart, and he motioned to them to take seats ; which they did.

And although he still sat with closed eyes, his family's feelings were sufficiently relieved to enable them to converse, in subdued tones, on indifferent subjects.

Mrs. Fane condescended to talk to Dolly and Florence, in this way leaving Winifred practically *tête-à-tête* with Mark. The girl, secretly a little attracted by his grave but gentle manner, began describing in a very animated and charming way a certain eccentric bibliophile whom she had known in Paris. This old man had talked to her by the hour on his beloved subject, enlarging on his frequent visits to the Quais, his baffled longings, his deluded hopes, his rare trouvailles of precious books which had escaped the lynx eyes of dealers. He told her how he had journeyed to Toulouse to see the collection of Count M'Carthy, and to Padua, there silently to adore a ' Catullus' on vellum. He abounded in anecdotes of book-collectors, past and present, from Bussy-Rabutin to Charles Nodier, and revelled in recounting how many tens of pounds, more or less, depended upon an infinitesimal difference in the margins of an Elzevir.

' What a delightful old monomaniac !' said Mark, looking with pleased interest at his companion's sparkling face. ' My father has not nearly so much enthusiasm. That is, I suppose he has it, but he does not show it.' As he pronounced these words, it did not escape his hearer's quick observation that there was a subtle change in his voice, and a curious unwilling doubt in the glance that he directed towards the venerable head in the velvet cap.

' Has Sir John a catalogue of his books ?' Winifred presently asked, her eyes ranging along the well-filled shelves.

' No, indeed. It is a great want. He is

always saying he must invite some capable person down to make one.'

' Then I know the very person for him,' exclaimed Winifred impulsively. ' Poor Dick Dallas.'

' And who is Dick Dallas ?' asked Mark. ' And why is he " poor "?'

' Because he is so unfortunate,' said Winifred : and she poured forth the story of Richard's wrongs.

'I do not think he would be at all the proper person for my father to employ,' observed Mark, when she had finished.

' Why not ?'

' A man who has been accused of culpable negligence, to call it by no harsher term——'

' But I tell you he is innocent,' flashed out Winifred.

' So you say, Miss Power, and you have possibly good personal grounds for believing it. But the rest of the world would unfortunately require proof,' continued Mark, with a touch of indulgent, smiling irony.

' Surely it is tea-time,' interrupted Sir John,
rising. ' I shall be glad of a cup. Did I hear
you say something, Miss Power, about a
person capable of making a catalogue of my
books ?' he inquired, as they went into the
drawing-room.

Enchanted at the question, Winifred a
second time recounted her tale.

' Try to persuade her that there are a few unfortunate people in the world who are not worth
helping,' said Mark, with a smile, to his father.

But Sir John, on the contrary, looked
tender, and took Winifred's hand in his.

' Your enthusiasm does you honour, my
child. Even supposing the young man to be
guilty, he should be given a second chance for
his own sake. You can write to Mr. Dallas,
if you like,' he resumed, after a pause of
thought ; ' tell him what the work would be,
and ask him to come here. He shall have his
board and lodging until it is completed.'

' And—and a salary ?' faltered Winifred.
She was almost speechless with joy and grati-

tude, but a vivid vision of the sorely-pinched Dallas household urged her to the question.

'Bless me, no!' exclaimed Sir John, with unusual briskness. 'We have imperative duties towards society, my dear young lady. One of these duties is the observance of discipline towards the erring. Until your friend has reconquered his position, he should be encouraged, but not indulged.'

Slightly crestfallen but still grateful, the girl expressed her thanks; she felt too exultant to mind even Mark's answering glance to her mother's low-toned remark:

'My dear daughter is almost Quixotically soft-hearted. Sometimes even I venture humbly to remonstrate with her.'

Later in the evening, when the guests were gone, and Sir John was again alone in his library, he was disturbed by the entrance of Mrs. Hatherley. He looked up at her quickly and not amiably, while she paused beside his chair. Evidently she had something to say, in the saying of which he would not help her.

'John,' she began at last, tremulously, 'you are kind to so many ; so kind. Have you no compassion for *him?*'

'Again, Laura ! How many more times must I beg of you not to speak to me on that subject ?'

'But he is starving,' whispered Mrs. Hatherley, and clasped her hands imploringly.

'He deserves to starve,' retorted Sir John. 'I tell you, for the fiftieth time, that I will not give you a penny for him. I do not wish to appear to cast what I do for you in your teeth, Laura; but you might, I think, sometimes count up the number of years you have been here, and what I have done for you and your daughters. How can you expect me to supply the extravagance of a spendthrift and a——an inebriate ?'

'He is your brother's son,' urged the mother, trembling with agitation.

'My *disinherited* brother's son,' was the cruel answer.

Could that be quiet Mrs. Hatherley who,

raising her brown, slender head from among her shawls, like a snake emerging from the grass, shot out at her benefactor a glance so full of venom?

'Why have you supported us all these years?' she asked

Sir John stared.

'I like that question, Laura! Out of kindness, of course.'

'Not because Mary bid you?'

'Mary! Now, understand me, Laura. I will submit to neither insolence nor insinuation. As long as you behave becomingly, the shelter of The Limes is yours; but it would cost me nothing to part from you to-morrow. How much it would cost you and your two empty-headed girls is another question.'

Mrs. Hatherley cowered as beneath an icy blast. To her poltroon creole soul, the bare idea of poverty and exertion was like death. She turned and crept away, humbled, silenced —but unforgiving.

Sir John followed her with his eyes as she

left, his attitude very rigid the while, his expression very hard. There was so little of the gentle student or the benevolent invalid in him at that moment that Winifred, had she seen him, would have been much strengthened in her distrust of the bland and gracious master of The Limes.

CHAPTER XI.

MRS. CHANDOS-FANE cultivated Sir John Hatherley's goodwill with an industry that was in no-wise lessened by his obvious insensibility to her charms. In point of fact, she was thinking that she should like to be Lady Hatherley, and that perseverance might eventually win the day. Perhaps she also thought that if she failed with the father, there was no reason why Winifred should fail with the son. Mark, indeed, seemed much the more likely prize. He evidently admired Winifred, and as evidently liked her. The great obstacle arose from the girl herself. She was so absolutely frank and uncompromising ; so devoid of coquetry ; so bent upon convincing rather than conciliating, that her mother was secretly in despair.

For the rest, she had her hands full : for if Sir John would not fall a captive to her bow and spear, there was another who would, and did. And that was Mr. Burton, the Rector.

He was a rich and childless widower, and one of those slow, heavy, honest men who think that no man can be expected to comprehend women. Their airs and graces, their nerves and fancies were to him just as recondite as their articles of costume. *They* recognised the wrong side of a mantle from the right, and pronounced the front of a bonnet to be its apparent back. It was to be presumed, consequently, that they knew also what they meant when weeping or blushing unaccountably, or saying one thing while thinking another. All a man had to do was to take things quietly as long as he was pro-

vided with his dinner. These being his ideas,
it may be imagined that he was wax in the
hands of a charming woman like Mrs. Fane.
It was a perfect comedy to watch his face
when she was talking to him, pouring out,
with her enchanting smiles and various waves
and nods of her pretty head, the clap-trap
second-hand ideas in which she delighted.
She talked to him of Baudelaire (of whom,
fortunately, he had never heard) ; of early
Italian art ; of stained-glass windows and the
degeneration of modern morals. Now he
thought he had understood her, now he was
afraid he hadn't ; now he had the dawn of a
suspicion that if he did, he would not approve
of her. But as she invariably wound up with
some sentiment of extreme propriety, he
would smile upon her, reassured that her
nimble intelligence had outstripped his stolid
one.

Still, the Rector of Elmsleigh could not
approach Sir John Hatherley in a worldly
point of view, and Mrs. Fane spent many an

evening in the drawing-room at The Limes ;
walking thither after dinner. Sir John, by
the light of a shaded lamp, sometimes dropped
majestically to sleep over some huge folio
while talking with her ; Dolly and Florence
played backgammon ; and Mrs. Hatherley
kept a stealthy and not too well-contented
watch upon Winifred and Mark.

They had drifted into the habit of talking
almost exclusively to one another. Mark, attracted by her frank friendliness, spoke more
freely to her than to most people. She learnt
with surprise that while Sir John was still
supposed to have a share in business operations of some magnitude, Mark was entirely
excluded from all knowledge of them. Unable
to remain idle, he had invested the little
fortune inherited from his mother in certain
mines, and occasionally made journeys to the
North in consequence. With her quick perception, Winifred divined that Mark felt the
distance at which his father kept him. There
was indeed a slight constraint between the

younger and the elder man. Mark, Winifred guessed, would have loved his father could he have fully understood him ; and he was studiously respectful and attentive to him always. But Sir John, while indulgent to his son in all respects but one, treated him with indifference. The one point on which he was not indulgent was money. Winifred was fain to confess that his generosity towards his relatives must repose on other (and, of course, higher) grounds than mere lavishness.

Indeed, for the master of such a house, and the reputed owner of such wealth, Sir John was careful to the verge of avarice. Mark was reduced to live strictly on his own income, and was too proud, as well as too experienced, ever to ask for more. Every art and subterfuge had to be resorted to by Mrs. Hatherley and her daughters before they could obtain money for their personal wants ; and of late it had even become a kind of joke among the tradespeople that Sir John would never pay a bill until the last possible moment.

Many a man besides Sir John has become miserly from immense wealth.

' He is beginning to get a little cranky,' people said, with an indulgent smile ; although, considering his heart-disease, he looked wonderfully handsome and vigorous.

Richard Dallas had accepted Sir John's offer with great promptitude, and a week or two later presented himself at The Limes. Winifred noticed with some pain that adversity had not improved him. He had grown cold and cynical, and without looking at all shabby as to coats, bore about him the signs of recent ill-fortune and privation. But he set to work at the catalogue with steadiness and intelligence, and Sir John was much pleased with him. Winifred was delighted : it was giving Richard the chance he needed.

So the days passed pleasantly. Richard hard at work by day, joining the drawing-room circle in the evening ; and sometimes walking out with the two young girls, generally by the side of Dolly.

'I hope they are not falling in love with one another,' thought Winifred. 'Sir John would not like that.'

When the catalogue was nearing completion, Sir John began to wonder how he should employ him next.

'I think I must send him to the Hague to purchase several very rare editions which I hear will shortly be for sale there,' he said one evening when Richard was not present. 'It is a question of spending some thousands, and therefore I must have an agent of intelligence as well as honesty on whom I can rely.'

'Mr. Dallas is certainly intelligent,' murmured Mrs. Fane, in a tone which implied that there was more doubt about the honesty.

Winifred flushed; and Mark, noting it, said chivalrously, 'My father seems to me to have made an excellent choice in employing him.'

'I flatter myself I understand character,' resumed Sir John. 'The young man tells me he has a sister who is at present in London seeking employment. She has been teaching in a school at Turin.'

Turin? Then it was Gertrude! Winifred and her mother exchanged glances.

' She would be willing, he thinks, to enter any family for nothing at present. I am thinking of engaging her to teach the girls French. They are still deplorably ignorant of the language—as I found when we were at Boulogne.'

The faces of the sisters fell considerably at this announcement. Winifred received it in silence; Mrs. Fane with an ironical smile. Gertrude! But they said nothing.

The next afternoon, when Winifred was busy painting in her studio, and her mother, seated at a little distance, was alternately pointing out faults in the picture and perusing a novel of De Goncourt, Richard Dallas arrived to pay a visit. Winifred received him warmly, as usual, but was quick to notice that he seemed ill at ease.

After a little desultory conversation, he said abruptly:

'Do you know that Gertrude is in London ?'

'So Sir John said,' answered Winifred gently.

'He is kind enough to wish her to be governess to his nieces. Winifred—Mrs. Fane, you will do nothing to prevent it ?'

He spoke entreatingly, with an earnestness and a feeling unusual to him. Touched, our impetuous Winifred had almost opened her lips to give the required assurance, when Mrs. Fane spoke drily.

'The responsibility of recommending your sister as a governess is yours, Mr. Dallas; what right have we to interfere ?'

Richard turned red. He was in the uncomfortable position of wishing them to be silent on the subject of Gertrude's escapade in Paris ; and desirous at the same time not to seem to attach much importance to the escapade itself. A perfectly scrupulous man might have hesitated, under the circumstances, before introducing his sister at The Limes. But perhaps Richard could not afford to be very scrupulous, and Gertrude's position touched and troubled him.

' She is all alone in London,' he said, pleadingly.

' Why did she leave Turin ?' inquired Mrs. Fane.

' She did not like the climate.'

Mrs. Fane pursed up her lips : most climates, in her opinion, would disagree with Miss Dallas.

Winifred meanwhile had been reflecting. After all, she and her mother knew nothing positive against Gertrude, for the suggestion thrown out by Hortense had never, so far as they were aware, been verified. Suspicions they might have, but suspicions were no ground for action. Moreover, all her warm young heart went out to the friend of her youth, and turning towards her mother she said :

'We must let her come.'

'You always do as you like, my love. And you know that I never say anything,' replied Mrs. Fane.

'You may depend upon our silence,' said Winifred to Richard. 'When will Gerty come?'

'Sir John has mentioned next week.' And with a few words of gratitude, Richard went.

Mrs. Fane went on reading for a little space in silence.

'When is Mark to be back?' she suddenly asked.

'Not for a fortnight, mamma.' Winifred was extremely surprised and angry with herself to feel how the unexpected question had brought a rush of blood to her face. She hoped her mother did not see it, and continued her painting in an agony of puzzled embarrassment. Mark had started for Scotland that morning on his usual business, and Winifred was missing him much more than she would have owned to herself.

'Then when he returns, Miss Dallas will already be installed at The Limes,' after another pause remarked Mrs. Fane.

'Well ?' said Winifred.

'I dare say he will admire her very much.'

Winifred mixed her colours with great accuracy; changed one brush for another; and began to work on another part of her picture before she replied. And then it was with an appeal.

'You will be kind to Gertrude, mother, will you not ?'

'I am not aware, my love, that I am ever deliberately unkind to anybody. I may be mistaken, of course, but I have never been accused of it, and I have had many tried and valued friends : although perhaps *you* would not have cared for them, darling.'

'I did not mean to offend you,' said the girl humbly. 'But I am anxious, *very* anxious' (with strong emphasis) 'that Gertrude should have a fair chance at The Limes.'

'I shall not interfere with her ; and you may be as Quixotic as you please. That's all, Winifred.'

So matters were arranged by Sir John with Miss Dallas, and she came to Elmsleigh to enter upon her engagement. With a shrinking which she did not care to analyze, Winifred allowed one clear day to elapse after her arrival before she went to see her.

She found her already installed in the schoolroom, with Dolly and Florence. Condemned to study again after their long period of liberty, they were both looking very doleful indeed.

Winifred entered with a beating heart, but was frozen on the very threshold by the coolness with which Gertrude rose to receive her.

'I will take you into the conservatory for a little chat when I have set my pupils their tasks,' she said composedly.

Winifred's sense of humour was greatly roused by the sight of the poor pupils. They had been vanquished, but a certain sulkiness betrayed their inward rebellion. When they presently brought their copybooks for correction, Gertrude, seated—a picture of elegance and beauty—in a luxurious armchair, took occasion to harangue them on the advantages of self-help, and to inform them that if they wished to learn anything thoroughly they must learn it unaided.

'My system is that you should do all that is possible without any assistance from me. Naturally you will make mistakes, but these mistakes, in course of time, will correct themselves. Here are your tasks for to-morrow,' indicating an appalling number of pages. 'I shall limit myself to explaining, when necessary, the principles to which you must find the particular applications.'

There was a pause; Florence began to cry. Then Dolly, a thought more spirited, said:

'I am sure my uncle will want us long before we have finished.'

'If Sir John really requires you, I shall give

you leave to go. But I shall tell him that I object to frivolous interruptions,' answered Gertrude calmly. Her pupils gasped.

'*Tell him!*' Dolly's exclamation died away helplessly; and, leaving them to their amazement, Miss Dallas swept out of the room and into the conservatory.

'I think it is rather a shame of you to put upon those two foolish little things,' exclaimed Winifred, with some heat.

'My dear,' said Gertrude, examining some japonicas with a critical air, 'I know what I am about. The experience of the last six months has not been thrown away upon me. I intend to play second fiddle in the world's orchestra no longer.'

Winifred was silent. She had expected some humility.

'I am young, and I think I may flatter myself neither stupid nor ugly,' continued Gertrude, turning her rings round her white fingers. 'Fate has been against me hitherto, but I shall try to rise superior to it in future.'

'Do you intend to work?' asked Winifred curtly.

'If necessary,' answered her friend. 'I have come here (and, by-the-bye, I ought to thank you, Winifred, for having been the means, through Dick, of securing me the place) to keep my eyes and ears open. In Paris, where, as you know, my life was one long toil, I was a failure. But all that is past. In future I hope to be successful.'

Winifred turned, thoroughly chilled and disappointed. Gertrude's vague boasts jarred upon her common-sense and her honesty. Almost she began to ask herself if she had been right in introducing her to The Limes. 'Good-bye,' she said, rather listlessly, as she held out her hand.

For a moment Gertrude's face wore a softer expression. 'You were always kind to me——' she began, when Winifred eagerly interrupted her. 'If you would only be true, dear!' she exclaimed, her cheeks flushing and her eyes kindling, as Gertrude yielded her hands to the clasp that had so warmly seized them.

Once more Gertrude's mood changed. 'Don't try to recall me to the sylvan glades of sentiment,' she said, with a light laugh and a shrug of her graceful shoulders. ' Those were all very well in our buttercup-days, but now our paths have diverged. You are a good soul, Winifred, but you must leave me to go my own road. I promise you not to do anything very base or mean. Cease to distress yourself, dear; I shall not be the less honest for not being '' goody.'' Good-bye.'

It was quite wonderful to see with what rapidity Gertrude obtained the upper hand of most people at The Limes as time went on. Her insolent beauty, her grace, her wit and self-possession compelled in Sir John a delighted, in the others a reluctant, homage. When Richard had departed for the Hague, she was installed the greater part of the day in the library, and set to write the notes and transcribe the memoranda that had formerly been the sisters' joy and pride. They, in the schoolroom now, inking their fingers and crying their eyes out over their verbs, relieved their feelings by private grumbling, but dared make no open protest.

Mrs. Hatherley grew daily yellower, thinner, more silent; Mrs. Fane daily more exasperated. The latter lady had indeed tried a passage-at-arms with the beautiful governess, but she came off second-best. She was no match for Gertrude. Next she tried what a little private aspersion would do with Sir John; but was quick enough to see that there was not much to be gained in that way. So she solaced herself by telling a great deal to Mrs. Hatherley, who listened eagerly and promised secrecy.

'Sir John is being completely hoodwinked,' she said to Winifred. 'I suppose Mark will be the next victim. Perhaps he will marry her. Then, I hope you will be satisfied, darling. She ought never to have come here.' Winifred listened in silence and pain.

When Mark returned, he did admire Gertrude very much; and, lounging away an hour in Winifred's studio one morning, he told her as much with infinite frankness of enthusiasm.

' You have got on famously with your work,' he said presently, changing the subject. 'That is a nice little head. Quite Southern too, in type. Was your model an Italian?'

' Only half Italian,' Winifred answered: and began to relate the circumstances. She was a young girl who had presented herself of her own accord to her one day, as a model, saying she came from London. While painting from her, the girl let out that her father, who was an Englishman, had formerly been a coachman in Sir John's service, that he was now bed-ridden, and he had sent her down to The Limes on a begging errand. She had been roughly received by Sir John, and apparently sent away empty-handed. And being of a timid disposition, she had hit upon the ingeni-ous device of offering herself as a model to Winifred, and getting *her* to intercede for the money.

17—2

'What a strange thing!' exclaimed Mark. 'How did she hear of you?'

'I don't know. At your house, I suppose; some of the servants may have gossiped with her. Her mother, an Italian, is dead: her father had married late in life, she said, after quitting Sir John's service.'

'What is the man's name?'

'Ridgeley.'

'Ridgeley?' mused Mark. 'I do not remember him. Perhaps he belongs to the Marleyford days, when I was a boy. They have faded from my memory in a great degree.'

'Then I am afraid that you also will be unable to tell me who Mademoiselle Marthe can have been,' said the girl, disappointed. 'I asked Sir John one day, but he apparently remembered nothing.'

Sir John, indeed, had seemed very much out of humour that day, and Winifred almost fancied—only of course it could only be fancy! —had been a little changed in his manner ever since.

' Who is she?' inquired Mark.

Winifred told him Mademoiselle Marthe's story, as much as she knew or guessed of it. He listened, interested in her warmth and evident conviction — interested, too, in her vivid description of the little old woman : but he could not throw much light on the matter.

' Your story recalls an incident which took great hold of my childish imagination,' he said. ' I remember just such a little woman as you describe, coming, like the malignant fairy to the princess's christening, an uninvited guest to Aunt Mary's wedding, and spreading dismay among us. I, a child, was dressed in some absurd costume as a page, and was holding up the bride's train. All at once this poor madwoman, who was, I fancy, a kind of a relative of ours, pressed her way through the crowd and stood looking about her wildly. And, now I come to think of it, her name was Martha also.'

' *Martha?*' Winifred dropped her brush

and turned to Mark with a startled face. For
she remembered that in her ravings Mademoiselle Marthe had called incessantly on
' Mary.'

CHAPTER XII.

THE idea which Mark had so unconsciously awakened took possession
of Winifred's mind. A hundred
times a day she cast it from her with horror,
but still it returned, strengthened continually
by her knowledge of Mrs. Russell's character.
Her devotion to her uncle had never availed
to blind her to the essential selfishness and
heartlessness of his wife. Winifred, with a
clearness of insight that came from her own
crystal candour, knew her for what she was—
shallow, self-indulgent, apathetic habitually,
and occasionally violent. Some faint sugges-

tions in Mademoiselle Marthe's ravings, dis-
regarded at the time, came back to Winifred
now with all the vividness of proof. Some
certainty she felt she must have ; she could
not live with such a suspicion and not seek to
dispel or to confirm it. Mark, she naturally
shrank from questioning, a vague instinct
warning her that the mystery whose veil she
was about to lift, probably involved Sir John
as well as his sister. The very notion of
some great committed wrong seemed more
probable to Winifred since she had known the
courtly owner of The Limes. Every day that
handsome face—so impassible and so pallid,
so rigid without real strength—had struck her
more and more as a mask. Every day she felt
more strongly the hollowness of the man ; his
vain theatricality, his thin pretensions to be a
student and a sage. And even stronger than
all this in her was the feeling that he was
fundamentally bad. By the very recoil of her
expectations regarding him, she had been
suddenly illuminated ; and coming fresh to

the scene, observant and penetrating as she was, she had felt the presence of a secret that fell like an invisible blight upon every member of the family.

That Sir John alone had the key to it, that it concerned him and nobody else, Winifred was sure. Even Mark only betrayed at times a vague perplexity; while as for Dolly and her sister, they simply remarked once or twice that of late 'Uncle John was somehow changed. Perhaps his heart was worse.'

He certainly complained very much oftener of that organ than of old; made more frequent visits to London to consult the specialists on the subject; and was more difficult to approach with any request for help or sympathy. On the other hand, his bibliomania greatly increased; and he was intensely interested in the results of Richard's trip to the Hague. The young man and he were in constant correspondence; and Sir John made frequent allusion to the number and value of the editions that he was buying.

'Does Dick like Holland?' asked Winifred

one evening of Gertrude, moved by a desire to say something amiable to her former friend, with whom she now rarely exchanged a remark.

' I believe so,' was the answer. ' But he does not write to me.'

' But then you see his letters to Sir John,' said Mrs. Fane.

' I beg your pardon. I conduct a great deal of Sir John's correspondence, but not that with Richard : I fancy he thinks I don't know how to spell " Elzevir," ' retorted Gertrude coolly.

' Nevertheless,' thought she to herself, ' it *is* odd, now I come to think of it, that he never shows me those letters. And he is rather mysterious about a good deal of his correspondence, though I would not admit it before these women for the world.'

' The member for Walford is dead, sir,' said Mark, a little later, to his father.

' So I see. Do you still intend to stand ?'

' I think so. I shall go to London to-

morrow, and then run down to the place itself
and set things *en train.* Of course I shall be
beaten, but even that is a beginning,' continued
the young man.

Winifred looked up quickly. So that was
why Mark had adopted no profession. He
intended himself for political life. She looked
at his broad brow, and his grave, resolute face,
almost as handsome as, and yet so different
from, Sir John's; and already her imagination
saw him in the arena victorious. He met her
glance, and while his own brightened at her
manifest sympathy, she dropped her eyes with
a sudden blush, and a sudden thrill that was
half shy and half delightful. She was rather
angry with herself for this emotion; and she
had never been in love. In her student days
she had regarded the ardent youths who adored
her with a scornful indulgence, half motherly,
half schoolboyish, that had sent them nearly
out of their minds.

Shortly after Mark's departure, Winifred
went to spend a week or two in London with

a young lady-artist whom she had known in
Paris. There, in the studio, she again met the
young model. She had reached that stage of
her picture when she required more models
than it was convenient to bring down to
Elmsleigh.

Among the most frequent of these was that
Mariuccia Ridgeley, the daughter of Sir John's
former coachman. She was a pretty little
thing, full of wilful ways and a fitful Southern
grace, and talked a great deat about herself and
her sick father.

' He is much worse,' she said one day, shaking her head mournfully. ' And the doctor
orders so many things that I cannot afford to
get him. He has written again to Sir John:
would the signorina mind asking if the letter
had been received ?'

Winifred had a great objection to asking
anything of the kind; and preferred helping
Mr. Ridgeley as much as she could out of her
own slender purse. She even tried to point
out to Mariuccia that the mere fact of having

been a coachman once in Sir John's service
did not entitle her father to be supported by
that gentleman for the term of his natural life.

'Ah! but Sir John has helped my father
often,' said Mariuccia. 'He used to send him
money whenever he asked for it, big sums—
ten pounds—twenty pounds——'

Winifred was greatly surprised. Of all the
perplexing people she had ever known, Sir
John was the most inscrutable. Just as she
had made up her mind that he was avari-
cious, some act of generosity on his part would
reach her. But one day the girl came with a
different request—that Miss Power would
kindly visit him.

'I really think he is dying,' she added.

It was a foggy afternoon when Winifred
turned her steps towards the man's lodgings.
They were in a street not very far from the
British Museum. Mariuccia gave her a glad
welcome, and ushered her into the little kitchen
where Ridgeley was sitting. She found him a
man of big, burly frame, that contrasted

mournfully with his evident weakness. He
was propped up by pillows in an armchair,
and it was evident that every breath he drew
was torture to him.

'I have to thank you, ma'am, for your kindness,' he began slowly, when Winifred was
seated, 'but I cannot afford much breath.'

She began some words of comfort, when he
stopped her with a gesture.

' There isn't much comfort for me now in the
world, miss. The best thing I can do is to
leave it. What I wanted to say was, will you
ask Sir John Hatherley for fifty pounds? I
don't want it for myself; but for *her*,' and he
nodded towards Mariuccia.

Winifred stared at him in speechless amazement. Was he mad, to ask for such a sum
and in such a tone? He was watching her
face quite coolly, and seemed fully to expect
an answer.

'I could not think of making any such request,' she said at last. ' And moreover it
would be useless.'

'I would not trouble you,' pursued Ridgeley, quite undisturbed by her refusal, 'but you see my hands,' and she noticed that they lay motionless and paralyzed. 'I cannot write myself, and I don't like to trust anybody else to *write*' (he laid a stress on the word) 'what I now have to say.'

'You must find some other messenger,' said Winifred. But she spoke gently, for speech had so increased his asthma that it was pain to sit and watch him.

'Nay, ma'am, you *must* speak,' he gasped, using the words not imperiously, but because he obviously was too weak to try persuasion.

'Tell him, please, that I say in the old days he was readier with his money; *and that he knows the cost of refusal.*'

'That sounds like a threat,' said Winifred haughtily.

'It is one,' Ridgeley answered.

More reluctant than ever now to undertake any such mission, she rose and turned to the door. The man, past all speech, looked at her imploringly, while his face turned of an ashen-grey, and his breathing filled the room with a grating sound, like the creaking of some cruel machine. All at once Winifred turned and again approached him, impelled by a new idea.

'Tell me,' she said, almost vehemently, as though conjuring his answer to find voice. 'When you lived with Sir John Hatherley, was there any member of his family called Martha?'

He bent his head in assent.

'And,' continued Winifred, beginning to tremble with excitement, 'did they do her any wrong?'

He made the same sign.

She stood looking at him, uncertain what to ask next, and possessed with a sudden scruple at what she had asked already.

He raised himself with an effort, and laboriously bringing out each word, as though it were wrung from the grasp of a vice, he whispered :

' Bring—me—the—money—and—before—
I—die—I—will—clear—Miss—Freake.'

Freake—Martha Freake! So that was the
name. With scarcely so much as the ceremony
of a nod to Mariuccia, Winifred hurried away,
feeling now that though the knowledge she had
wanted was hers, she had gained it by unworthy means. What right had she to spy
into Sir John's past? The question presented
itself to her for the first time, and she realized
at the same moment how completely possessed
she had been by the suspicion that had filled
her mind for days. She wished she had never
gone near Ridgeley; she almost wished that
she had never known Martha Freake.

In much turmoil of feeling, Winifred returned to Elmsleigh, her visit being over.

One of Mrs. Chandos-Fane's peculiarities
was that she always opened her daughter's
letters. Winifred had entered one or two
protests, but as she did not really prize her
correspondence very highly, the only letters
that she ever insisted on keeping to herself

were her uncle Walter's. And fortunately,
these Mrs. Chandos-Fane did not care to read:
they were too clever for her. She opened one
(in a strange handwriting) the morning after
Winifred's return.

That same evening at The Limes, Mr. Bur-
ton not being there to absorb her attention,
Mrs. Fane lost herself in contemplation of Sir
John, who had not pleased her of late. Sir
John had sat for some time in deep reflection,
rubbing his white hands softly one over the
other, when he broke silence by addressing
Miss Dallas.

' Did I tell you your brother had returned
to Paris ?'

' Indeed ?'

' Yes. He has transacted my business
really admirably at the Hague. I was greatly
pleased with his letter this morning.'

Mrs. Hatherley here audibly sighed. The
last letter she had received had been a demand
(the third) for immediate payment from her
dressmaker; but although she had left the

open bill on Sir John's table, he had taken no notice of it, and draw his attention to it more openly she dared not.

Unfortunately the word 'letter' had awakened an association also in the mind of Mrs. Fane.

'Winifred had a strange letter this morning,' she remarked. 'Did you tell Sir John about it, my dear?'

Winifred's blood froze in her veins. The letter had been from Mariuccia, asking, on her father's part, if the message concerning the money had been given. What, in the name of all that was tactless, did her mother mean by speaking of it?

'What was there to tell me?' asked Sir John sharply.

Winifred plucked up heart of grace. Something she would tell him, and perhaps his answer would disperse her doubts. 'My letter was from a girl—a model, Sir John. Her father, Ridgeley, was once in your service. He wishes you to help him.'

In a pause that ensued Mrs. Hatherley turned pale with annoyance. Another applicant, while every request of hers was refused !

' How much does Ridgeley want ?' asked Sir John raspingly. ' Of *course* money is the object of his message. I know what this kind of application means.'

' He is ill,' said Winifred. ' Very ill indeed.'

' Well ?—how much ?'

' Fifty pounds.' Winifred wondered if her heart-beats could be heard through the silence.

Sir John gave a short, sarcastic laugh. ' This Ridgeley was an honest fellow enough, but he has been unfortunate,' was his observation. ' I may give you a cheque for him to-morrow, Miss Power ; but I trust I shall have no other application of the kind from you.'

The cheque, enclosed in an envelope directed to herself, was duly delivered into her hands next morning by one of the footmen of The Limes. It was for fifty pounds.

Winifred, astounded at the generosity, re-
solved to carry the money herself : it would
not take her long to run up to London and
back : and she started without loss of time.
On reaching her destination and climbing to
the top of the house, she was struck with the
stillness within. Generally Mariuccia's voice
was to be heard blithely singing ; but now
there was not a sound. She knocked, and the
girl came herself to open the door. She was
weeping violently, and on recognising Winifred, exclaimed, ' Oh ! signorina, you are too
late. He is dead.'

' Dead !'

Softly following the grief-stricken girl,
Winifred entered the bedroom. A little
stunned, she sat down, and holding Mariuccia's hand, stroked it softly in silent
sympathy.

' It happened late last night,' sobbed
Mariuccia. ' He was sorry to go, but sorry
only for me. He said I was to tell you something which he never told while he was alive,

for fear of punishment—but now it does not matter who knows.'

Involuntarily Winifred's grasp tightened round the hand she held. 'Yes. Go on, child.'

'I was to say that Sir John and his sister and my father once perjured themselves to spare Miss Hatherley disgrace, and they got Miss Freake sentenced to imprisonment, and all because she knew too much about Sir John's marriage.'

The words, interrupted by tears, but repeated with a quiet indifference like a lesson learnt by rote, for a moment made Winifred feel dizzy. Recovering, she poured forth a string of rapid questions, but Mariuccia could not answer them. 'That was all he said,' she repeated mournfully, then laid her head down, and let her sobs break out afresh.

'Are you alone?' asked Winifred, when she rose to go.

'Some of the neighbours look in,' Mariuccia replied listlessly. Winifred took a sovereign

out of her own purse and laid it upon the
table. She had the cheque in her pocket, but
without Sir John's consent, she did not feel
justified in giving so large a sum to the girl
so promising future help, if needed, she went.

She had plenty to think of as she walked
through the streets. The possibility of doubt
no longer remained to her, and she was in a
white heat of indignation at Sir John. She
would not stop amid such dishonest people,
she said impulsively; she would go away
from Elmsleigh.

She remembered the quiver of passionate
resentment with which she had listened to
Martha's ravings in the fever, and condemned
in her heart the unknown wrong-doer who
had wrecked that innocent life. Was she to
be less severe now that she knew who the
wrong-doer was? Then, with a quick catching of her breath, a sudden sharp pang, she
thought of Mark, and unconsciously quickened
her step.

In the high-strung mood produced by these

meditations, Winifred reached home. On entering the little drawing-room, she found Mrs. Fane sitting alone in the blaze of the fire-light, apparently lost in thought. Another time Winifred might have noticed the quick, rather excited way in which she looked up on her daughter's entrance; but the girl was too much absorbed in her own feelings. She suddenly leant her head down against her mother's knee, while her eyes filled with an unexpected rush of tears. The tears Mrs. Chandos-Fane did not see, but she gently moved her daughter's head away, saying :

'Take care, my love. I have on my new dress.'

'Have you been out?' Winifred asked, sitting upright, her eyes quite dry again.

'Yes. Mr. Burton has had a really delightful afternoon tea.'

'Delightful ?'

Winifred had a vivid, rapid vision of the old maids principally composing the party; of

Mr. Burton, rubicund and complacent in the midst of them; and of all the gossip, from mild to malignant, talked. ·

'*I* thought so. Of course, it was all very conventional ; so, perhaps, you would not have enjoyed it. I do not complain of you, my love. Of course, there are things that I should like to change in you, but—ah, well! it's no matter.'

' Dear mother!' exclaimed Winifred, feeling rather disconcerted.

'I never grudged you to my suffering brother—never,' resumed Mrs. Fane, as if struck with the recollection of her own magnanimity. 'I resigned you cheerfully ; for those who know me best have never thought me selfish. But I am not strong-minded— and pushing—and masculine ; and it is not to be wondered at, I think, if I sometimes feel lonely.'

At this point of her self-analysis, she produced her pocket-handkerchief ; Winifred was fairly melted.

'Dearest mother! I am so sorry—I never thought—I never dreamed——'

'I don't complain, my love. I have said so before. You are rather wilful and head-strong ; you have a harder nature than mine. How should you understand what I was feeling ?'

'But in future I will try to understand. We will be more to one another,' faltered Winifred, honestly wondering where her fault had been.

'Too late !' said Mrs. Fane, shaking her head impressively. 'You should try to bear in mind, dear, that " there is a tide in the affairs of men." Who says that ? Some charming poet, I am sure. If we let that tide ebb, we are stranded. Your poor little mother is called to a higher duty. I am going to be married.'

Winifred gave a gasp.

'Mamma! To Mr. Burton ?'

'Yes, dear. I feel how unworthy I am of him. But I cannot resist the temptation of a little happiness, and I have promised to be his wife. The wedding, for reasons of Mr. Burton's, is to be immediate. You must sacrifice your painting for once to mamma, and assist me with the trousseau.'

And Winifred was too much astonished to say more.

After dinner she went round with her mother to The Limes, making up her mind that it should be her last visit. She would return Sir John his cheque, and just tell Mark how sorry she was that he had lost his election. He had returned that day, defeated. It was only natural that she should assure him of her sympathy with his disappointment.

Mark came forward to meet her with a pleasure very quietly displayed, but of which she had learnt to read the signs. He cut short her condolence by saying, with a smile, that he never expected to be victorious, and added:

'I am so glad to be back, that the election seems like a tiresome dream.'

He spoke with a grave, significant tenderness, but she did not respond by so much as a glance.

On the contrary, she turned away abruptly, determined not to unclose her heart to a hope that, once admitted, might choke all her valiant resolutions. She had done with the Hatherleys, and could make no exceptions: that was what she told herself.

Sir John was sitting, as usual, a little apart, and crossing the room with a swift step, Winifred paused beside his chair. He looked up at her with some surprise, struck, perhaps, by her pallor and the light of suppressed excitement in her shining eyes. She took the cheque from her pocket, and handed it to him.

'Ridgeley is dead,' she whispered in low tones ; and if her suspicions had needed any further confirmation, she would have found it in the brief but unmistakable flash of relief that illumined her hearer's face.

He took the cheque from her in silence, still

keeping his eyes fixed on her, but more, she fancied, in defiance than in inquiry.

' He has left his daughter in great poverty,' continued Winifred.

' I have nothing to do with his daughter,' was the frigid reply.

' If he did not prosper, it was perhaps because of his wickedness,' said Winifred.

She began to tremble as she spoke, all the smouldering indignation within her again catching flame.

' Was he wicked ?' Sir John carelessly asked.

' If you consider wickedness that which you all did to poor Martha Freake.'

Winifred had hardly spoken the words, when Sir John rose from his chair and confronted her with a glance of scathing contempt. She recoiled from it as from a blow.

' You have come to my own house to insult me, Miss Power !'

The reproach was not unmerited, and Winifred felt it. She had spoken in the impulse of temper, and would have given worlds now to recall her words. Sir John had spoken distinctly; it was heard by the others in dismay; they gathered round.

'What is all this?' exclaimed Mark.

Sir John spoke up. 'It is this,' he said haughtily. 'Many years ago, a member of our family, Martha Freake, disgraced herself by writing anonymous threatening letters for the purpose of extorting from me a sum of money to cover an act of culpable negligence, if nothing worse, on her own part. She was brought to trial for it—it could not be avoided—and sentenced to a short term of imprisonment. But ere she entered on it, reason failed her, and she was transferred from prison to an asylum. I paid for her there, and would have continued to maintain her after her recovery and dismissal, but she rejected my offers and went to live abroad. I had never expected to be reminded of her, in the manner of to-night. But Miss Power, who appears to have a liking for the society of models and of

servants, has been exercising their lively, if
not exalted, imaginations at my expense :
armed with the startling information acquired
in this underhand way, she seeks by deliberately insulting me to vindicate the character of
a maniac and do the bidding of a coachman.'

Everybody turned to look at the object of
this denunciation. She stood perfectly still,
very pale and grieved, but not subdued.

'I do not understand,' exclaimed Mark,
angry and perplexed.

'Nor I,' added Mrs. Fane's dulcet tones.
' But if my poor dear child has been so unfortunate as to offend Sir John——'

' Please, mother, do not try to set things
right,' Winifred interrupted steadily. ' For
the manner of my offence I ask Sir John's
pardon. The feelings which impelled me to
my unfortunate speech are not so superficial
that a word can dispel them. But I can at
least promise, and I do, never to obtrude them
on anybody here again, for this is my last visit
to The Limes.'

She turned in her impetuosity and walked straight away from the room and the house.

They had all been too much astonished to stop her. Gertrude was the first to speak—good-naturedly.

'That is Winifred all over. She is a fine creature, but often in heroics.'

'Do pray excuse her, Sir John,' added Mrs. Fane. 'Dear Mrs. Hatherley, you don't know my impulsive, good-hearted girl.'

Mrs. Hatherley did not answer. Her eyes had a strange glitter, and she looked uncommonly wide awake.

Nobody else spoke, and the silence became at last so oppressive, that Mrs. Fane was fain to break it with a lady-like outburst of sobs.

At the first sound of these Sir John vanished to the library, Mark followed him, and Florence was made happy by being asked to bring her smelling-bottle to the rescue.

Winifred meanwhile, in the darkness and solitude of her own sitting-room, was sitting by the spent fire, and weeping her heart out in the mere physical reaction of her late excitement. She felt angry with herself, yet not altogether sorry. At the sound of the door-bell she roused herself, thinking that it must be her mother, and nerved herself for a scene. But to her great surprise, who should walk in but Dolly, panting, and in a remarkable state of excitement.

' Oh, dear Miss Power,' she exclaimed, sinking breathlessly on to a stool at Winifred's side, ' I hope you will excuse me, but I came because I really felt I must. Everybody is so angry at The Limes—Uncle John shut up in the library—Mark looking *dreadful*—your mother in tears. She says perhaps you will be going back to Paris.'

' Did she say that?'

' Yes. And I want you—if you do go—to take me with you.'

' And what in the world would you do in Paris ?' asked Winifred.

' Paint plates and fans and things,' replied

Dolly promptly. 'Painting in water-colours is my one small talent.'

Winifred smiled with melancholy amusement. She had often suspected that Dolly was not quite such a nonentity as her sister, but she had not been prepared for an outburst like this, and wondered what had inspired it.

'Do you want to get away from your governess, Dorothy?'

'No — that's not it ; not altogether. I should like to be independent, to earn money.'

Winifred shook her head as she looked down at the small daintily-dressed figure, and the pink-and-white, pretty, Dresden-china face.

'Oh, don't discourage me, dear, *dear* Miss Power!' exclaimed the girl, clasping her hands, with tears in her eyes. 'When Uncle John dies I am convinced that we shall be paupers ; he will be sure not to leave us anything. I will be no burden to you. I will live on bread and water, I will sweep your rooms, I will——'

'Hush! If there be any way of managing your enterprise, I will not discourage it, you may be sure. But indeed I do not know what I am going to do. Dolly, answer me frankly—have you no other motive for wishing to go than this, and the general weariness of life at The Limes?'

Dolly was very honest. She hung her head in silence.

'Am I to flatter myself that you are inspired by affection for *me?*' continued Winifred playfully.

'I like you very much.'

'But somebody else better?'

Again Dolly was mute.

'Well, well,' said Winifred, laying her hand on the pretty little head, 'I will bear you in mind. And meanwhile (just to amuse you, you understand), I will read you a letter from Richard Dallas.'

END OF VOL. I.

BILLING AND SONS, PRINTERS, GUILDFORD AND LONDON.
G., C. & Co.